D#320490

D1603771

Utah People
in the
Nevada Desert

Utah People
in the
Nevada Desert

*Homestead and Community
on a
Twentieth-Century Farmers' Frontier*

Marshall E. Bowen

UTAH STATE UNIVERSITY PRESS
Logan, Utah
1994

Utah State University Press
Logan, UT 84322-7800

Cover Design by Mary Donahue

Library of Congress Cataloging-in-Publication Data
Bowen, Marshall E., 1938–
    Utah people in the Nevada desert: homestead and community on
    a Twentieth-century farmer's frontier / by Marshall E. Bowen.
    p. cm.
    ISBN 0-87421-168-9 (acid-free)
    1. Wells Region (Nev.)–History. 2. Frontier and pioneer
life–Nevada–Wells Region. I. Title.
F849.W45B68   1994
979.3'16–dc20   93-44996
                                                                      CIP

To My Parents
Hazel and Everett Bowen
Who Pointed Me in the Right Direction

Contents

Illustrations

Preface

THIS IS AN ACCOUNT OF A SMALL NUMBER OF TWENTIETH-CENTURY PIO-
NEERS who moved from their homes in northern Utah to the desert and
semidesert lands of northeastern Nevada. It analyzes the processes that interacted to produce this movement, describes the economic and social life that
developed in the new settlements, and identifies the migration streams that
these people followed when things did not work out in Nevada. By concentrating on fewer than two hundred households, it permits creation of an intimate portrait of colonization during a time when people throughout the
American West were trying their hands at homesteading in extremely marginal lands. At this scale, the men and women who participated in this
movement can be seen as individuals, with personalities, values, and lifestyles that are not hidden within a mass of impersonal data. But investiga-
tion at such a microscopic scale does not mean that widely applicable lessons
cannot be learned from the experiences of these people. Indeed, the scope of
this study permits us to see beyond ordinary analytic parameters, and to recognize the importance of personal decisions in the settlement process, of individual farming procedures, and of interactive social forces at work during
the years of outmigration.

This study relies on a wide variety of sources, some of a standard nature
and others that are less commonly used. In the first category are numerous
Utah and Nevada newspapers, which not only provide a running account of
events described in the chapters that follow, but also yield, in local news col-
umns written by rural correspondents, valuable information that makes it
possible to discern individual threads in the fabric of life in these small communities. Manuscript collections, particularly those of the Nevada Historical
Society and of the Mormon church, whose Metropolis Ward Historical Record is a particularly rich source, serve a similar purpose. These materials are
supplemented by information gleaned from manuscript census returns, city
and county directories, local tax records, and railroad land department files.
Interviews with elderly settlers and their children provide insights to pioneer
life that would have otherwise escaped notice.

An extremely valuable source, seldom utilized by scholars working in this field, is the collection of forms and other papers that every early twentieth-century homesteader was required to file with the General Land Office in order to obtain legal title to property. These documents, formally designated as "Serial Patent Files" and commonly known as "Homestead Patent Applications" (HPAs), are the property of the National Archives. They include personal information about the individual applying for ownership, a detailed description of improvements completed on the homesteader's land, and a year-by-year account of acres cultivated, crops planted, and yields obtained from the time a homestead was occupied until the settler applied for a patent. The applications are supplemented by the statements of two "witnesses" (usually neighbors), who described the improvements made by the applicant and provided additional information about their family ties (if any) with the applicant and the length of time that they had been acquainted. Many of these files also contain correspondence between applicants and the General Land Office, and between homestead inspectors and their supervisors, which clarify points made in the original applications, provide additional details about applicants' farming activities, and describe the length and cause of settlers' absences from their claims. One exceptional file contains an eighty-four page court transcription, supplemented by letters, affidavits, and reports, all pertaining to the contested application of a Salt Lake City man who settled in Independence Valley, southeast of the town of Wells. This set of documents, which includes lengthy statements by almost every person who lived in Independence Valley for more than year, supplies a wealth of information about the settlers themselves, their activities before moving to Nevada, and their lives in the valley. When combined with the sources described in the previous paragraph, these and the other General Land Office files give distinctive identities to most settlers, and bring the details of the everyday lives of ordinary people into sharp focus.

This work has benefited greatly from the assistance and encouragement of many individuals who helped to smooth the way from its inception to completion. Howard Hickson, director of the Northeastern Nevada Museum, who first introduced me to the phenomenon of early twentieth-century settlement in his part of the state, and provided work space during several stages of this project, deserves special mention. Shawn Hall, the museum's assistant director, has been extremely helpful in tracking down photographs of the Metropolis area. My thanks also go to the staffs of the Utah State Historical Society, the Nevada Historical Society, the special collections of the libraries at the University of Nevada and Utah State University, the Historical Department of the Church of Jesus Christ of Latter-day Saints, and the National Archives, particularly its Washington National Records Center in Suitland, Maryland, who all located obscure materials, gave insightful advice, and provided encouragement during the years spent acquiring the information presented here. Numerous old-timers, in particular Gene Pengelly, Will McDaniel, Opal Troxel, and Cliff Jensen, graciously agreed to be interviewed, patiently endured my questions about matters that seemed perfectly obvious to them, and, through long hours of conversation, succeeded in conveying to me some of the spirit of pioneer life in the Nevada desert. Without their help, I would never have succeeded in narrowing serious gaps in my understanding of the settlement process. Mary Washington College awarded generous Faculty Development Grants that enabled me to travel to research facilities in Utah, Nevada, and California. Mary Washington's fine cartographer, James Gouger, produced all maps and graphs, for which I shall be eternally grateful. John Alley of the Utah State University Press has been a constant source of encouragement and has provided sound editorial advice. Finally, I give special thanks to my wife, Dawn, who gladly took time from her own work on northern Canada's agricultural frontier to encourage me and to volunteer insights derived from her research and who tolerated, with patience and good humor, my use of the dining room table as a writing desk over the course of many long months.

Chapter One

The Framework

THE GREAT BASIN REGION ENCOMPASSES MORE THAN TWO HUNDRED THOUSAND SQUARE MILES of the western United States, extending from the Wasatch Mountains of Utah to the Sierra Nevada, and from California's Mojave Desert to the lava flow country of eastern Oregon. Except for its margins, most of the region is a monotonous succession of dry flats, separated at intervals of ten to fifteen miles by prominent north-south trending mountain ranges. Anyone traveling across the Basin can see that little of it is suited for farming. Indeed, more than a half-century after Mormon pioneers began cultivating fields near the region's eastern edge in 1847, less than one percent of its total area had been occupied by farmers.[1] But in the first years of the twentieth century, several interrelated forces drew thousands of agricultural settlers into this nearly vacant land, particularly the sagebrush-covered plains that stretch from Utah across northern Nevada into Oregon. The actions of these people constituted a brief but important chapter in the evolution of the West, and were, in turn, closely connected to political, social, and economic conditions in existence throughout the country at this time.

Settlement of these marginal lands was encouraged by a combination of circumstances that made utilization of the Basin's meager land and water resources seem desirable. Four new pieces of Federal legislation paved the way. The first was the Carey Act of 1894, authorizing the Secretary of the Interior to turn over up to one million acres to each of eleven western states for development of state-directed irrigation projects. Eight years later Congress further encouraged irrigation by passing the Reclamation Act, strongly supported by President Theodore Roosevelt, which decreed that funds derived from public land sales in sixteen arid and semiarid states could be spent on

1

the selection and survey of potentially irrigable land and for the construction of dams and canals that would bring water onto the land. As soon as this bill was passed, Roosevelt and the U.S. Geological Survey organized the U.S. Reclamation Service, charged with implementing the provisions of the Act.[2]

Dryland settlement was stimulated when Congress, responding to the Progressive policies espoused by Roosevelt, passed the Enlarged Homestead Act of 1909, giving settlers 320 acres of unirrigable land instead of the usual 160-acre quarter section. Amendments made to this Act in 1912, which reduced the residence requirement from five years to three, allowed absences of five months each year, and lowered the cultivation requirements from one-fourth to one-eighth of a settler's total acreage, removed some of the more difficult barriers imposed by the original Act and appeared to bring ownership of a viable dry farm within reach of anyone who expended a reasonable effort. The spirit of the Enlarged Homestead Act was continued in 1916 with passage of the Stock Raising Homestead Act, which awarded a full section of land to settlers who lived on their claims for three years and made improvements valued at $1.25 per acre.[3] None of these laws guaranteed that settlement in the Great Basin would be successful, but together they offered fighting chances, at low cost, for people who sought to establish farms of their own.

An upsurge of interest in dry farming went hand-in-hand with the new homesteading regulations. Westerners had been investigating ways to farm dry land without irrigation for years, and by the early 1900s they had developed a set of principles for what became popularly known as "scientific dry land farming." These tenets, calculated to help farmers maximize their utilization of limited amounts of precipitation, included deep plowing, thin sowing, thorough cultivation of the soil, and summer fallowing. The emphasis placed on this latter procedure, whereby only half of a farmer's cultivated land would be put in crops each year, had initially made full-fledged adoption of dry farming impractical in most parts of the Great Basin, but with passage of the Enlarged Homestead Act, settlers were finally able to obtain units of sufficient size to make this method appear economically attractive.[4]

Utah led the Great Basin in the development and promotion of dry farming, with remarkable successes recorded in Cache Valley, about eighty miles north of Salt Lake City. Here, the work of practical farmers was supplemented by experiments at the state agricultural college in Logan, whose staff provided numerous educational services for dry farmers and was instrumental in establishing six experimental dry farms in outlying parts of the state. One of these, near Nephi, was later selected by the U.S. Department of Agriculture as the site for its own studies of dry farming possibilities in the Basin.[5] The region's other states lagged behind Utah in their support of the dry farming movement, but by 1909 Nevada had begun to catch up by creating the State Agricultural Experiment Dry Farm in Pleasant Valley, south of Elko. Two years later Oregon established a dryland experiment station of its own near the town of Burns in the southeastern part of the state.[6] Combined with the proven success of dry farming in northern Utah, the presence of these stations in the midst of sagebrush lands being eyed by prospective settlers lent tangible support to the notion that the farmers' frontier could be pushed a little closer toward the Basin's arid heart.

The region's railroads also contributed to the growing interest in agricultural settlement. Dozens of nearly unoccupied valleys were penetrated in the early 1900s by construction of the San Pedro, Los Angeles, and Salt Lake line through the western Utah desert and by the Western Pacific, built from Salt Lake City across Nevada to California. Lesser lines, begun as feeder and connector routes, brought additional areas within reach of prospective farmers.[7] All of the new railroads sought to attract settlers to areas served by their tracks, but none outdid the Western Pacific, which organized specially discounted homeseekers' excursions to various points in Nevada and declared shamelessly that some of the most depressing flats along its route were in fact fertile, well-watered valleys with almost unlimited opportunities for farmers.[8]

The Southern Pacific, which had become the Basin's foremost trunk line through its takeover of the Central Pacific tracks and land grant, introduced still another dimension to the settlement process. Between 1910 and 1913 the railroad reclassified more than a million acres of its Utah and Nevada holdings from the category of "grazing land" to that of "agricultural land" and put the property on the market. The absence of restrictions on the amount of railroad land that a purchaser could obtain appealed particularly to real estate speculators, who bought up large parcels, subdivided them, and offered them for resale to prospective farmers at substantial markups. The tactics employed by some of these people tarnished the image of the region's real estate business, but promoters did succeed in attracting additional homeseekers to desert basins that might otherwise have escaped notice.[9]

None of the forces described above would have had much impact without the existence of a strong demand for new lands to farm. It was more than coincidental that these events were occurring during the peak of a nationwide

"Back-to-the-Land" movement and at a time when prices for farm products were rising sharply. City dwellers were encouraged by the movement's literature to escape their congested surroundings and start new lives in the country, where they could breathe fresh air, raise their children in wholesome social environments, and, perhaps most important of all, have places of their own.[10] The economic advantages of owning a farm were magnified when the price of wheat nearly doubled between 1898 and 1909 and then shot upward following the outbreak of the First World War. These considerations appealed to rural and small town residents as well as city people, and made developing a piece of virgin land, even in the Great Basin, appear to be a reasonable strategy for improving the quality of a person's life.[11]

Three parts of the region became particularly important targets for settlers responding to these inducements. Near the western rim of the Basin, the U.S. Reclamation Service began to develop the Newlands Project, designed to direct water from Nevada's Carson and Truckee rivers to a broad flat east of Carson City, where it was thought that 400,000 acres could be put under irrigation. Construction work began in 1903, and progressed rapidly as hundreds of men were hired to push the job to completion. By 1906 water was running into the fields; more than six hundred settlers, including a considerable number of Californians, were living on the project; and the town of Fallon was developing in the midst of newly reclaimed farmland.[12]

To the north, more than a thousand homesteaders and their families invaded Oregon's Fort Rock Valley, while others poured into the desert plains south and west of Burns. Although no systematic analysis has been made of these settlers' origins, it is clear that most of them came from various points in the Pacific Northwest, with Portland and Seattle, Oregon's Willamette Valley, and the wheat country of southeastern Washington supplying the largest share. A few of the lucky ones succeeded in obtaining ground water for irrigation, but the vast majority had to rely entirely on dry farming methods and bravely set about to transform these sagebrush-covered flats into lands of wheat, rye, and other small grains.[13]

Five hundred miles away, settlers began to occupy the vacant lands of western Utah. One of the most important movements took place 125 miles southwest of Salt Lake City, where several hundred prospective irrigators occupied a pair of Carey Act projects laid out on a stark desert plain near the town of Delta. Other pioneers, lured by the words of imaginative real estate promoters, established dry farms on dozens of remote flats between the Escalante Desert in southwestern Utah and the Idaho state line. At first, settlers came from points that literally spanned the continent, but after a brief sift-ing-out period, people from Utah became the dominant element, with most newcomers claiming the area from Salt Lake City to Cache Valley as their former place of residence.[14]

As the tide of agricultural settlement continued to rise, some of its waves swept beyond the borders of Utah into adjoining states. In northeastern Ne-vada, seven new farmers' communities, each settled in large part by trans-planted Utah people, came into existence between 1909 and 1915 within a fifty-mile radius of the small town of Wells (Fig. 1). Altogether, nearly two thousand men, women, and children made their way into these new settle-ments, with Metropolis, located a short distance northwest of Wells, ac-counting for the largest share. In spite of their common Utah roots, these places exhibited significant differences in the manner of their settlement, in the expectations and experiences of their residents, and in the nature and rate of their eventual disintegration. Examination of the four communities closest to Wells—Metropolis, Afton, Tobar Flat, and Independence Valley—pro-vides an excellent opportunity to understand, at the grass roots level, how these circumstances developed and to recognize that the movement of twen-tieth-century pioneers to and from the Great Basin's marginal lands was by no means a uniform process.

Study of these four communities also provides a local context for under-standing some of the broad themes of early twentieth-century agricultural settlement on marginal lands in the American West.[15] It enables us to see details of the Back-to-the-Land movement in action, to feel the stress and anguish that pioneers experienced as they struggled with a harsh, unforgiv-ing land, and to sharpen our appreciation of how social forces affected pat-terns of frontier life and landscape. But the meaning of this study transcends the local scene. By examining a small number of men and women trying to transform an obscure corner of Nevada into a land of farms and farmers' towns, we can discover valuable clues about the connections between nature, human nature, and the settlement process that may well have applicability for marginal lands throughout the West. A local study thus becomes a re-gional one, helping us understand how communities developed and then fell apart in this vast land of rugged mountains and raw desert plains.

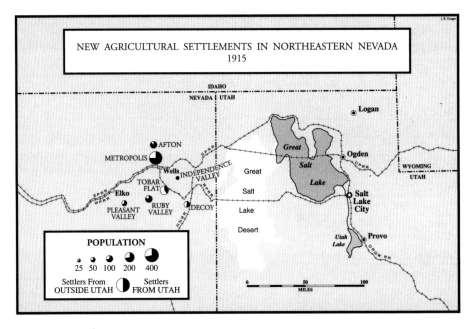

Figure 1

Chapter Two

The Settlement Process

High Desert Country

A visitor to Wells needs to venture only a short distance out of town to see that northeastern Nevada contains a variety of natural landscapes, none of them particularly favorable for farming (Fig. 2). Northwest of Wells, where Metropolis and Afton were established, gently rolling, sagebrush-covered plains which seem to resemble a vast but irregular gray-green sea stretch toward the horizon. Small but permanent streams flow toward the Humboldt River, and steep-sided gullies, barely visible from a distance, provide an unexpected element of diversity. Soils here are moderately fertile, provided moisture is available, but their productivity is often diminished by sheet erosion, which occurs with discouraging regularity during the spring runoff and after midsummer thunderstorms.[1]

No one would consider the Metropolis-Afton area a farmers' paradise, but it clearly holds more promise for agriculture than the country southeast of Wells, where Tobar Flat and Independence Valley occupy the bed of a long-extinct Pleistocene body of water known as Lake Clover. Here, mountain-born streams dwindle and finally expire in dull alkali flats, sagebrush gives way to greasewood, and low dunes rise above an otherwise featureless plain. With few exceptions, soils on the Lake Clover plain are poor. Some contain heavy concentrations of alkali, others are cursed with hardpan deposits just inches beneath the surface, while still others tend to drift whenever the wind blows. Even the most casual observer would agree with the conclusion of a government report, written more than a half-century ago, which declared that the Lake Clover plain is not a good place for farmers, and that much of

it, from the homestead country southwest of Tobar to the heart of Independence Valley, is no better than low quality sheep range.[2]

A unifying element, common to both settings, is light and variable precipitation. Long-term records indicate that annual precipitation in the vicinity of Wells averages about ten inches, and that years when only seven or
eight inches are recorded are not at all uncommon. April, May, and June are
ordinarily the wettest months, and July, August, and September are the dri-
est, but this pattern is not repeated year after year. In a land where each drop
of moisture is more precious than it would be in humid regions, the stalling
of a rain-producing front in the upper Humboldt basin or the failure of a
thunderstorm to materialize over Tobar Flat can be the difference between a
"wet" year and a "dry" one, or between "normal" and "abnormal" seasonal
conditions. In both 1913 and 1914, for example, Wells received about eight
inches of precipitation, well within its customary range. More than forty percent of the 1913 total fell, as expected, between April first and the last day
of June, but in 1914 only sixteen percent of the total was recorded during
these months, while July, August, and September, in complete contradiction
of long-term norms, accounted for more than a quarter of the year's precipitation. Winter snows usually provide close to half of the annual precipitation, but here, too, averages can be misleading. At the Metropolis weather
station, ten miles northwest of Wells, approximately 5.5 inches of precipitation, almost all in the form of snow, were recorded between November 1,
1913 and February 28, 1914, more than seven times the amount that fell
during the same four months a year later.[3]

Problems caused by moisture deficiencies are compounded by cold
weather and extreme temperature variability. Because of the altitude of the
area's valleys, which lie between 5,500 and 6,000 feet, freezing weather can
be expected until the first of June, and ordinarily returns around Labor Day.
The "normal" growing season, as measured from the last killing frost in
spring to the first one in fall, is about 100 days. But averages, once again, are
less meaningful than the extremes. In 1910 the growing season on Tobar Flat
lasted from April 30 until September 26, a total of 149 days, but two years
later it was just 81 days, from June 16 to September 5. In 1918 it lasted only
64 days. Even in midsummer, below-freezing weather is not unknown. At
Wells, a reading of 26 degrees was made on July 14, 1913, almost three
years to the day after the station's all-time high of 104 degrees was recorded.[4]

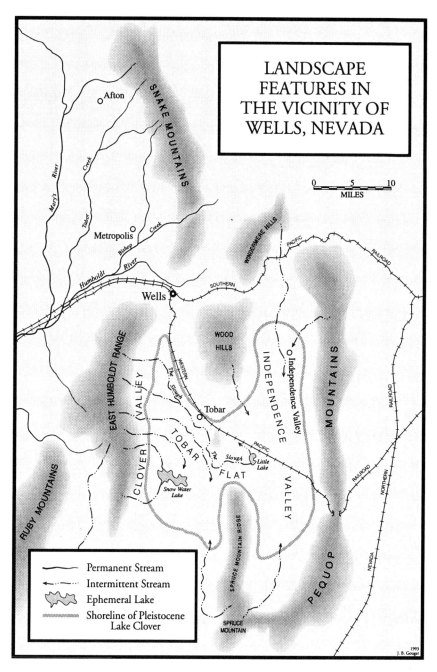

LANDSCAPE
FEATURES IN
THE VICINITY OF
WELLS, NEVADA

Figure 2

Figure 3. Section-line road in sagebrush country two miles north of the Metropolis canal. (Photograph by the author)

Figure 4. Dry channel of The Slough, the largest watercourse on Tobar Flat. View is downstream, toward the Pequop Mountains. (Photograph by the author)

Despite these environmental impediments, the elevated plains of northeastern Nevada were scenes of considerable settlement activity during the first years of the twentieth century. Participants in these events included land sharks and land-hungry homesteaders, city people and country folk, prospective irrigators and would-be dry farmers. Mormons were prominent in some communities and almost entirely absent in others. Only two elements were common throughout the area under study: each settlement had a strong Utah component in its population, and none had enough water to support large-scale colonization. These two dimensions—Utah people and high desert conditions—are the threads that connect this story of settlement and life in the valleys near Wells and provide a structure for analyzing the complex processes at work in the Great Basin at this time.

MIGRATION TO METROPOLIS AND AFTON

Settlement of Metropolis and Afton was directly tied to a large-scale promotional scheme that included plans for both irrigation and dry farming. The project's origins can be traced to 1903, when the mercantile firm of M. Badt and Company of Wells purchased the U-7 ranch on Bishop Creek, north of Wells, from one of the area's original pioneers. This acquisition gave the Badt family legal title to about ten thousand acres, including a nearly continuous strip of hay meadow below the ranch headquarters, scattered outlying tracts, and a promising but undeveloped reservoir site in a canyon east of the ranch, as well as control of an additional thirty thousand acres of railroad and public land that had been fenced by the U-7.[5]

Initially, the Badts intended to continue using the U-7 property for ranching, as they had done with similar purchases south of Wells, and they made tentative plans to increase the production of irrigated hay by constructing a small dam and reservoir in the canyon. These modest intentions changed abruptly in 1909, however, when they were approached by Harold L. Siegel, a promoter who operated a speculative mining business from his family's Salt Lake City clothing store, with a proposal to build a much larger dam and develop the property as part of a Carey Act colonization project. Siegel had become acquainted with the Badts and their land during visits to Wells while enroute to his Nevada mining properties. He viewed involvement with a real estate development here, near the main line of the Southern Pacific, as a splendid opportunity to replace the uncertain business of dealing in mining claims with a potentially more lucrative venture. The Badts agreed to sell the property to Siegel if he could secure the financing needed to develop such a project, which, it was thought, would cost at least a half-million dollars. It took Siegel less than a year to obtain the funds, principally from Jewish investors on the east coast, and to form the Pacific Reclamation Company, with Joseph Gutman of New York City as president and Siegel as treasurer and general manager. The New York firm of Paskus, Cohen, Lavell, and Gordon was retained to look after the company's legal affairs. In July, 1909, the company bought all U-7 properties lying north of Wells and made the reservoir site, the original ranchstead, and the downstream hay fields—about two-thirds of the total purchase—the cornerstones of its development project.[6]

The company's next step was to secure legal control of property that the U-7 had been using but did not own. This objective was largely achieved between August, 1909, and May, 1910, when the federal government turned over approximately ten thousand acres of public land to the state of Nevada for use by the company under provisions of the Carey Act. The acquisition included a small tract adjoining the original purchase in Bishop Creek canyon, needed for construction of the large dam proposed by Siegel, and a vast expanse of sagebrush country extending to a point about eight miles west of the old ranch headquarters. While these negotiations were taking place, the company also concluded a deal with the Southern Pacific for purchase of more than ten thousand acres of railroad land at $4.25 an acre, which it paid for in cash in May of 1910.[7]

In the summer of 1911 the company's plans were beginning to take shape (Fig. 5). By this time Siegel and his associates had added another five thousand acres of railroad land to the project, giving them control of approximately fifty square miles between the reservoir site and the western extremity of their holdings. Construction of the dam, said to consist in part of San Francisco earthquake rubble, was well underway, directed by a Salt Lake City contractor, and stakes marking the route of the main irrigation canal were in the ground. Four miles west of the U-7 ranch house, surveyors were platting a mile-square townsite, to be called Metropolis, and work was beginning on a two-story, fifty-room, brick hotel. To the southwest, railroad men were laying an eight-mile spur track that would connect Metropolis with the Southern Pacific main line.[8]

Already, the company's promotional arm had moved into action. With an eye toward recruiting Mormon settlers, whom he considered industrious, sober,

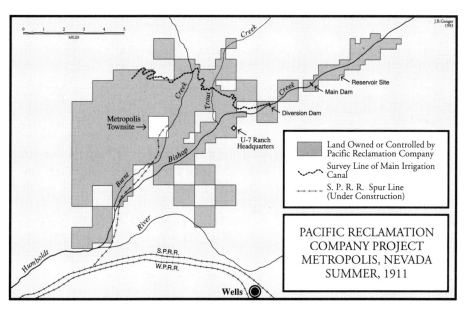

Figure 5

and more likely than others to pay their installments for land and water, Siegel opened sales offices in Salt Lake City and Ogden, and placed J. Wilford Woolf, a twenty-eight-year-old Mormon, in charge of the company's promotional campaign. Woolf was a native of Hyde Park, in Cache Valley, but had spent most of his life in Canada, where he had been elected to the Alberta legislature, and it was expected that his connections with the former place, his prominence in the latter, and his outgoing nature would help attract Latter-day Saints (LDS) to the new project. Woolf's assistant was John B. Crapo, a forty-year-old Mormon with Idaho roots who had formerly served as a colonization agent for the Canadian Pacific railway.[9] There is no direct evidence of formal LDS church involvement in the project, but a rumor that some of its leaders were privately advising people to try their luck in Nevada was blown up by Siegel and his associates into a published report that church authorities in Salt Lake City were full-fledged supporters of the company's scheme.[10]

One of the first steps taken by Woolf to attract buyers was the preparation of an attractive booklet describing the project in highly flattering terms. Soils around Metropolis, declared the booklet, were remarkably deep and rich, free of stones and alkali accumulations, and capable of producing a wide variety of crops. More than enough water would be available by early 1912 to irrigate ten thousand acres, and for those who preferred to buy dry farm land, precipitation approaching fourteen inches a year guaranteed certain success. Wonderful yields of irrigated vegetables were reported from the company's demonstration farm, and dryland wheat was said to average nearly fifty bushels to the acre. The company boasted that apples it had entered in a fair at Ogden had been awarded first prize against competition from four western states. All this, said Woolf, could be obtained for prices ranging from $55 to $75 for an acre of irrigated land and from $10 to $15 per acre for dry farm land, with ten percent of the total due in advance and the remainder payable over a period of ten years at six percent interest.[11] What the booklet failed to mention was that the vegetables had been raised in a long-established garden at the U-7, which now served as the demonstration farm, that the dry farmed wheat had undoubtedly benefited from seepage from nearby irrigated fields, and that the prize-winning apples had in fact come from a ranch south of the Humboldt River, some twenty miles from Metropolis. The rainfall figure announced by the company was at best a rough guess based on fragmentary records kept at the dam site and had nothing to do with actual conditions on the lands earmarked for dry farming.[12]

Figure 6. Hotel Meropolis nearing completion, early 1912. (Photograph courtesy of the Northeastern Nevada Museum)

Figure 7. Southern Pacific railroad depot at Metropolis, 1912. (Photograph courtesy of the Northeastern Nevada Museum)

Newspaper advertisements followed a similar approach. The *Metropolis Chronicle*, published by the company in Nevada but distributed in Utah as well, told its readers that eighty-five thousand acres would soon be under irrigation, that the company was seeking men "who are heeding the call of 'Back to the Soil'" as well as experienced farmers, and that "the most impressive part of the whole project is [its] stability." Calling its development "one of the greatest investment opportunities in the entire West," the company offered town lots for sale at $100 apiece, and boasted that the "variety of business opportunities open at Metropolis is unlimited."[13] Advertisements placed in Salt Lake City and Ogden papers proclaimed that Metropolis lay "in the heart of one of the richest and most fertile agricultural districts in the intermountain west," and urged Utah businessmen to "run over to Metropolis" to look into its investment possibilities. Prospective purchasers were offered round-trip excursions to Metropolis from Salt Lake City and Ogden at rates of less than ten dollars each.[14]

The excursions occurred at regular intervals from the spring of 1911, when the company's Carey Act property was put on the market, through the end of the year. Ordinarily, Woolf or Crapo met the parties in Salt Lake City or Ogden and accompanied them on the five- to six-hour journey by train to Metropolis, filling them with stories of the prosperity that awaited them if they bought company land. Upon their arrival, the visitors were taken to the townsite to see the progress being made on construction of the hotel and other buildings, entertained at the U-7, and shown some of the available farm land. Then they were transported to a well-developed ranch south of Wells, in which Woolf had obtained a part-interest, where they were fed a good meal and given the opportunity to complete purchase agreements with one of the company's agents. After an overnight stay in Wells, the travelers returned home, in many cases quite satisfied with the opportunities that seemed to beckon them back to Nevada.[15]

This campaign paid almost immediate dividends. In the late summer and fall of 1911, the company announced that it had already sold land to thirty men and women and that numerous others were on the verge of signing sales contracts. Nearly half of the purchasers had also filed dryland homestead claims, with six taking land in the vicinity of Metropolis and the remainder selecting property fifteen miles to the north, where the community of Afton would soon develop. Of these thirty individuals, twenty were residents of the Ogden area, four were from Cache Valley, and two others, from Star Valley, Wyoming, and Cardston, Alberta, were former residents of Cache Valley.[16]

Not all of these people would actually move to Nevada, but the pattern exhibited by their addresses at the time of purchase is a clear indicator of the direction from which most interest in the project was coming.

Land sales continued at a brisk pace into the spring of 1912. During this time, the hotel and several stores were opened for business, construction of the dam neared completion, and settlers were reportedly arriving at Metropolis at the rate of one family per day. By June, at least sixty families had moved onto company land.[17] Meanwhile, landseekers had also filed nearly a hundred quarter-section homestead claims, with slightly more than half located near Metropolis and the others at Afton. Some of these claims, as noted earlier, were made by purchasers of company land, but fully three-quarters were filed by people who were attracted to the area by publicity surrounding the project and elected to take their chances on cheap government land beyond the canal instead of paying the company's asking price. Another thirty-nine entries were filed between July, 1912, and the end of 1915, usually on property originally claimed in 1911 and early 1912. The majority of these new claimants moved onto land already abandoned by some of the first settlers, but about a dozen purchased relinquishments from people who had earlier claimed homesteads as investments, and held them until the demand for farms had pushed the market value of unimproved sagebrush land to unheard-of levels.[18]

During the first months of settlement, nearly a thousand men, women, and children moved to Metropolis and Afton. Approximately half of them, upon discovering that the company's claims had been greatly exaggerated and that serious legal problems threatened full-scale irrigation development, quickly departed, but by late 1912 the area's population had levelled off at about 450, a number that would remain more or less stationary for the next five years.[19]

The overwhelming majority of these settlers were Utah people (Fig. 8). Examination of the previous places of residence of 116 family heads and single adults who occupied company farmlands and outlying homesteads before the end of 1915 shows that fully seventy-five percent of them had moved directly from homes in Utah, with people from Weber County and Cache County far in the lead. Most settlers from outside Utah had come from Wyoming and Alberta, and of these, more than eighty percent had been born in Utah but had moved away with their parents in the 1880s, when the pressures of overpopulation and federal antipolygamy measures had forced hundreds of Mormon families to leave the state. Altogether, nine of every ten

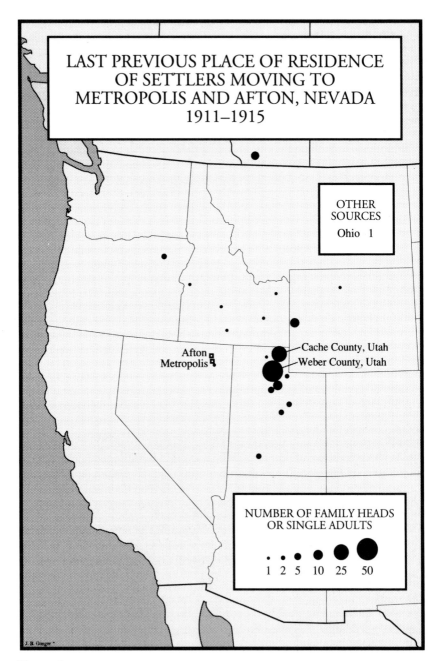

LAST PREVIOUS PLACE OF RESIDENCE
OF SETTLERS MOVING TO
METROPOLIS AND AFTON, NEVADA
1911–1915

OTHER
SOURCES
Ohio 1

Afton
Metropolis

Cache County, Utah
Weber County, Utah

NUMBER OF FAMILY HEADS
OR SINGLE ADULTS

1 2 5 10 25 50

Figure 8

settlers arriving at Metropolis and Afton between 1911 and 1915 were either residents of Utah or former residents of the Beehive State.[20] Predictably, all but a tiny handful were members of the Mormon church, an accounting confirmed by local observers, who have estimated that between ninety-five and ninety-eight percent of the area's settlers were Latter-day Saints.[21]

Typically, the male settlers from Utah were close to the prime of their lives, married, and the fathers of several children. Analysis of church, census, and homestead records reveals that their median age upon arrival in Nevada was thirty-four, and that only a quarter of them were older than fifty or younger than twenty-five. Eighty-six percent were married, and of the single men, exactly half were individuals in their early twenties who came to Nevada with parents or other relatives but occupied homestead claims of their own. Two-thirds of the married couples arrived with three or more children. Only seven married men were childless, and of these, four were newlyweds who had moved to Metropolis or Afton shortly after their marriages. At the other extreme, three men each arrived with a wife and ten minor children. Only four single women—a widow and a divorced woman, each with teen-aged sons, and two unmarried women in their thirties, both related to other settlers—were among the pioneers from Utah who obtained land of their own.[22]

It is possible to determine the previous occupation of almost every adult who moved to Metropolis and Afton between 1911 and 1915 (Table 1). About sixty percent had been engaged in agricultural pursuits at their previous places of residence, in all but one instance as farmers or farm laborers. Several were carpenters or masons, initially attracted to Metropolis by construction activities at the townsite, who chose to remain in the area and try their hands at farming. Most of the others represented typically blue-collar occupations such as railroad or factory work, general unskilled labor, and employment as teamsters.

For men in these latter groups, the appeal of the Back-to-the-Land movement must have been immense. It is easy to understand, for example, why people such as John Murrish, a forty-four-year-old father of eight, living in a rented house and working as a teamster at a Cache Valley sugar mill, or Oscar Geertsen, a thirty-two-year-old Ogden carpenter with five children, would decide that they could create better lives for themselves and their families by moving to the sagebrush plains of Nevada. Their viewpoint is clearly expressed by the words of the daughter of a railroad machinist from Salt Lake City, who remembered that "not in their wildest dreams" could her

TABLE I

PREVIOUS OCCUPATIONS OF MEN MOVING TO METROPOLIS AND AFTON, NEVADA, 1911–1915

	Settlers from Utah	Settlers from Outside Utah	Total
Farmers[a]	47	11	58
Carpenters	6	0	6
Railroad Workers	5	0	5
General Laborers	4	1	5
Factory Workers	3	1	4
Blacksmiths	2	0	2
Masons	2	0	2
Teamsters	2	0	2
Teachers	2	0	2
Clerks	1	1	2
Others[b]	3	3	6
Totals	77	17	94

[a]Includes nine farm laborers and one sheep herder, all from Utah.
[b]Includes a miner, a house painter, and a shoemaker from Utah and a barber, a butcher, and a deputy sheriff from outside Utah.

parents, both natives of Norway, ever hope to own so much land (148 acres) unless they took a chance on homesteading near Metropolis.[23]

Land hunger also affected many individuals who were already engaged in agriculture. Of the forty-seven Utah men counted as "farmers" in Table 1, at least eight were renting their land, nine were landless farm laborers, and one earned a precarious living by herding sheep. The renters' situation is well illustrated by the predicament of Philip Ferrin of North Ogden, who in 1910 had been married for twelve years and had five children, but had not yet been able to purchase a farm close to home. The farm laborers were no better off. Although a few of them worked for their parents, most were employed on other men's farms, in some cases on a part-time basis. For all of these individuals, a move away from familiar surroundings, even to the Nevada desert, seemed to be the most practical way to obtain places of their own.

It is less certain why men who already owned farms in Utah would decide to start anew in Nevada. There is no evidence that these people were experiencing poor crop yields in Utah, and reports of a church squabble in one community and an outbreak of scarlet fever in another do not seem sufficient causes to have sent so many of them out to the desert.[24] In all likelihood the principal incentive was an opportunity to obtain several times more land than they could possibly accumulate in Utah. Examination of the amount of land owned by these farmers at the time of their migration to Metropolis and Afton shows that the median size of their Utah holdings was about twenty-five acres and that no more than a quarter of them owned more than fifty acres. Several had less than ten acres each. In Nevada, by combining forty acres of company land with a quarter-section homestead, they could easily acquire two hundred acres, and if they could induce friends or relatives to secure additional parcels, it was possible to increase the property at their disposal to several hundred acres. Ownership of such relatively large tracts would also make it possible for some men, who had been growing fruit or raising dairy cows on small acreages, to switch over to commercial grain farming, which required substantially larger amounts of land. At a time when wheat prices were rising, becoming a grain farmer made sense, and for many, this goal seemed well within reach on the broad Nevada plains.[25] Still, the decision to move was not always based on economic factors. In many cases, personal considerations outweighed economic motives, a view expressed by a former resident of Bountiful, who explained that in 1911 several of his friends and relatives were moving to Metropolis, "and like a foolish man I followed them."[26]

The role of community and kinship, as suggested above, cannot be overestimated.[27] Certain small northern Utah communities contributed a disproportionately large share of the settlers, while other places sent few if any people to the Nevada frontier (Fig. 9). Half of the pioneers from Weber County were residents of either Plain City or North Ogden, while several others came from places only two or three miles distant from this pair of communities. Almost forty percent of the settlers from Cache Valley had been living in Hyde Park, the hometown of J. Wilford Woolf, the Pacific Reclamation Company's principal colonization agent, compelling evidence in itself that personal connections played critical roles in deciding which families would move to Nevada.

Examination of the linkages between settlers from these communities shows that migration to Metropolis and Afton was anything but a random

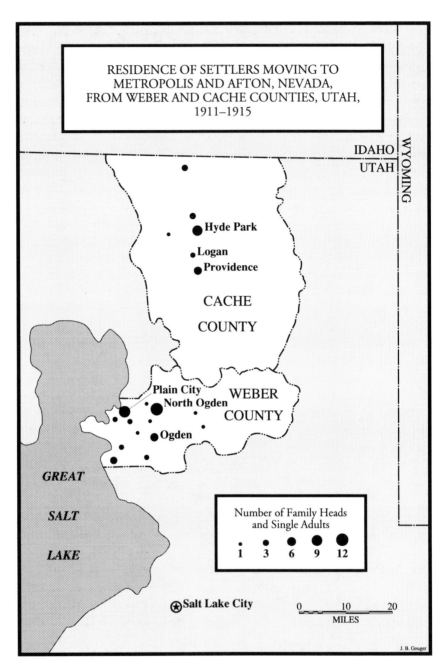

RESIDENCE OF SETTLERS MOVING TO
METROPOLIS AND AFTON, NEVADA,
FROM WEBER AND CACHE COUNTIES, UTAH,
1911–1915

IDAHO
UTAH

WYOMING

Hyde Park

Logan
Providence

CACHE
COUNTY

Plain City
North Ogden
Ogden

WEBER
COUNTY

GREAT

SALT

LAKE

Number of Family Heads
and Single Adults

1   3   6   9   12

⊛ Salt Lake City

0   10   20
MILES

J. B. Gouger

Figure 9

affair. The migrants were almost always friends and relatives of one another, ordinarily guided by a few influential persons. A principal catalyst at Plain City was John W. Luckart, a fifty-two-year-old dairy farmer whose sons, Raymond and Charles, joined him in the move to Nevada (Fig. 10). Charles apparently convinced his wife's father, William H. Miller, to come along with them, while the senior Luckart brought in Alma M. Thueson, whose small farm was separated from his own by just one house. A second Plain City network included Joseph F. Hutchinson, Sr., two of his sons, and Joseph F. Rawson, an unmarried farm laborer who lived nearby. There is no evidence of direct links between the Luckart and Hutchinson networks or that Margaret C. Arbon, a forty-six-year-old divorced mother of five, was either a relative or close neighbor of the other settlers, but in a small Mormon community like Plain City, with fewer than a thousand residents, all of these people were undoubtedly well aware of one another's plans to move to the Metropolis area.[28]

Connections between residents of Plain City who moved to Nevada carried over to those from North Ogden, six miles to the east, with both networks in the former place linked to those in the latter. One set of contacts extended from Mrs. John W. Luckart (the former Ada Shupe) to Mrs. Sarah Shupe, a widow who lived right next door to Adna Ferrin, and to William G. Shupe, a forty-nine-year-old blacksmith. Ferrin was related by marriage to William M. Ellis, a carpenter, whose son, Charles, was a son-in-law of Thomas F. Brown, a farmer who worked regularly on threshing crews organized by Samuel S. Ferrin, Adna's brother. This network continued by way of Philip Ferrin (brother of Adna and Samuel) to Philip's neighbor, John A. Hall, another carpenter who often worked with William M. Ellis, and to Thomas W. Norris, a young brick mason whose residence was a short distance from Hall's home. A second connection between the two communities involved William H. Hutchinson of Plain City, who was a friend (and future in-law) of the family of Alma L. Montgomery; Alma's widowed cousin, Mrs. Deseret C. Storey; and Benjamin F. Blaylock, Jr., whose wife was Alma's sister. Evidence that Blaylock, Mrs. Storey, Adna Ferrin, and the Ellises were good friends who traveled together to Nevada brings the two North Ogden networks into close alignment with one another and further supports the premise that personal relationships were critical elements in the settlement process.[29]

Similar links connected all of the settlers from Hyde Park and led directly to a large number of other people who also settled near Metropolis (Fig. 11). Here, the network began with the brothers George and Alma Balls and three

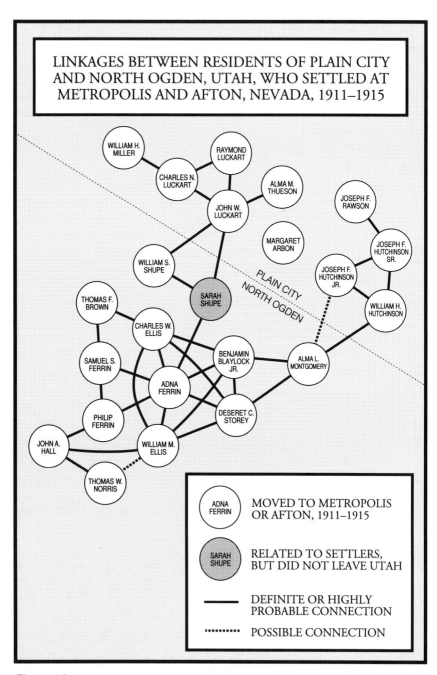

LINKAGES BETWEEN RESIDENTS OF PLAIN CITY AND NORTH OGDEN, UTAH, WHO SETTLED AT METROPOLIS AND AFTON, NEVADA, 1911–1915

WILLIAM H. MILLER

RAYMOND LUCKART

CHARLES N. LUCKART

ALMA M. THUESON

JOSEPH F. RAWSON

JOHN W. LUCKART

MARGARET ARBON

JOSEPH F. HUTCHINSON SR.

WILLIAM S. SHUPE

JOSEPH F. HUTCHINSON JR.

THOMAS F. BROWN

SARAH SHUPE

PLAIN CITY

NORTH OGDEN

WILLIAM H. HUTCHINSON

CHARLES W. ELLIS

SAMUEL S. FERRIN

BENJAMIN BLAYLOCK JR.

ALMA L. MONTGOMERY

ADNA FERRIN

PHILIP FERRIN

DESERET C. STOREY

JOHN A. HALL

WILLIAM M. ELLIS

THOMAS W. NORRIS

ADNA FERRIN — MOVED TO METROPOLIS OR AFTON, 1911–1915

SARAH SHUPE — RELATED TO SETTLERS, BUT DID NOT LEAVE UTAH

—— DEFINITE OR HIGHLY PROBABLE CONNECTION

·········· POSSIBLE CONNECTION

Figure 10

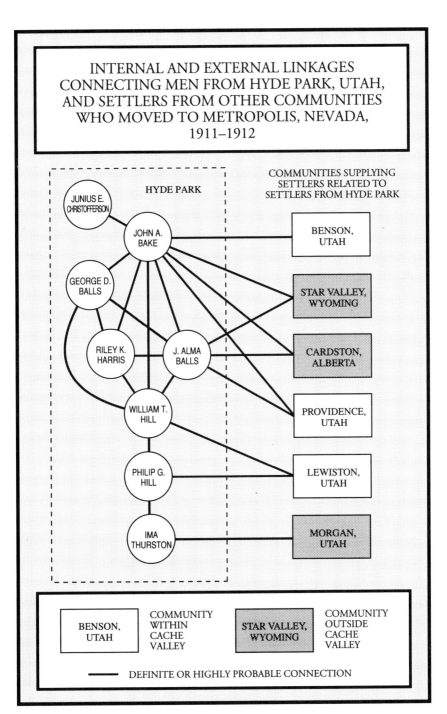

INTERNAL AND EXTERNAL LINKAGES
CONNECTING MEN FROM HYDE PARK, UTAH,
AND SETTLERS FROM OTHER COMMUNITIES
WHO MOVED TO METROPOLIS, NEVADA,
1911–1912

HYDE PARK

COMMUNITIES SUPPLYING
SETTLERS RELATED TO
SETTLERS FROM HYDE PARK

JUNIUS E. CHRISTOFFERSON

JOHN A. BAKE

GEORGE D. BALLS

RILEY K. HARRIS

J. ALMA BALLS

WILLIAM T. HILL

PHILIP G. HILL

IMA THURSTON

BENSON, UTAH

STAR VALLEY, WYOMING

CARDSTON, ALBERTA

PROVIDENCE, UTAH

LEWISTON, UTAH

MORGAN, UTAH

BENSON, UTAH

COMMUNITY WITHIN CACHE VALLEY

STAR VALLEY, WYOMING

COMMUNITY OUTSIDE CACHE VALLEY

——— DEFINITE OR HIGHLY PROBABLE CONNECTION

Figure 11

of their brothers-in-law, Riley K. Harris and William T. Hill (married to sisters of George and Alma) and John A. Bake (married to a sister of Alma's wife). It extended in one direction to Hill's father, Philip G. Hill, and from Philip to his next-door neighbor, Ima Thurston, and in another direction to Junius E. Christofferson, a young farm laborer who lived with his aunt on property adjoining the Bake place.[30]

Family ties also joined people from Hyde Park with settlers from at least six other predominantly Mormon communities. Philip and William Hill, for example, were related by marriage to Charles W. Hanline, a settler from Lewiston, while Ima Thurston was a second cousin of Roy Thurston, who moved to Metropolis from the vicinity of Morgan. Links extended from Hyde Park to Providence through Bake and Alma Balls, whose wives were sisters of the wife of Horton H. Hammond of Providence, one of the first settlers at Metropolis. Through a complex set of interrelationships that included existing and former marriages, first and second cousins, uncles, nephews, and half-brothers, both Alma Balls and John A. Bake were also related to J. Wilford Woolf and several settlers from Alberta, as well as to the Hydes (including four sons of the founder of Hyde Park) and three other families who moved to Metropolis from Star Valley, Wyoming. A final connection also involved Bake, who was married to the daughter of George Lyon, a farmer from Benson. These family relationships led, in turn, to other relatives and friends of relatives who came from as near as Cache Valley and as far away as eastern Oregon.[31] Through this sometimes confusing maze of kinship and community connections, one fact remains perfectly clear: very few people set out for the Metropolis-Afton area without knowing several other individuals who had already moved to Nevada, or would soon be on their way.

This sense of community continued into Nevada. All but two of the settlers from Cache Valley, including everyone from Hyde Park, occupied land near Metropolis, while the Plain City and North Ogden people tended to gather at Afton. Although incomplete company records and the practice of some people to live considerable distances from the land they were farming makes it impossible to precisely reconstruct residential patterns at Metropolis, it is obvious that most settlers chose to live near relatives and old friends. Six of the eight families from Hyde Park had homes within a mile of one another, with four occupying homesteads in the same section, while four of the five settlers from Providence lived just a little more than a mile apart. The people from Star Valley (in almost every instance related to settlers from

Hyde Park) also clustered together. No one from Star Valley lived more than a half-mile from another settler from Star Valley or someone from Hyde Park, and in one area north of the townsite a solid block of nearly three square miles was occupied exclusively by settlers from Hyde Park or Star Valley.[32]

The tendency of friends and relatives to establish homes in the same neighborhood was clearly demonstrated at Afton (Fig. 12). In the summer of 1915, Afton contained twenty-nine occupied dwellings housing approximately a hundred people. At least twenty-three of the community's family heads were former residents of Utah, with sixteen having previously lived in Weber County. All of the settlers from Weber County were congregated within five miles of each other, with a large number clustered near the home of John W. Luckart, the community's most prominent citizen, who farmed, operated a general store, and served as Afton's postmaster and justice of the peace.[33] Three other Utah people, all relatives of one another, lived about a mile north of the Luckart place. Several miles to the south, near the road to Metropolis, were the homes of two families from Cache Valley and one from Salt Lake City. Here, too, the settlers were linked by long-standing personal ties, for the wife of the Salt Lake City man was a sister of the wife of one of the men from Cache Valley. These circumstances, in existence from one end of Afton to the other, further reinforce the notion that patterns of settlement in this part of the Nevada desert were largely extensions of kinship and community networks that had originated years before in Utah.

UTAH SETTLERS ON THE LAKE CLOVER PLAIN

While these events were taking place at Metropolis and Afton, other settlers were filtering into the dry lands southeast of Wells, where their efforts led to the establishment of two new communities, Tobar Flat and Independence Valley, on the broad bed of Lake Clover. More than half of the people who arrived in this area before the end of 1915 came from Utah, with the overwhelming majority originating in Salt Lake City and its immediate environs (Fig. 17). In contrast to the colonists at Metropolis and Afton, only a handful had been residents of the Ogden area or Cache Valley, very few had been farmers, and a much smaller proportion were members of the Mormon church. But like the settlers northwest of Wells, these people were tied together by links that had been forged in Utah, and most of them would take

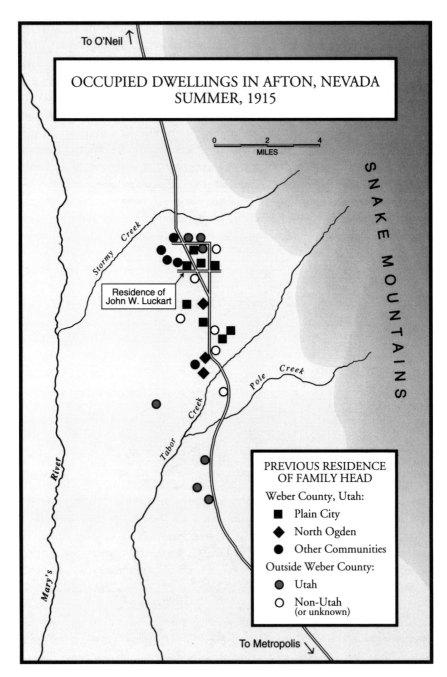

OCCUPIED DWELLINGS IN AFTON, NEVADA
SUMMER, 1915

0   2   4
MILES

To O'Neil ↑

SNAKE MOUNTAINS

Stormy Creek

Residence of
John W. Luckart

Pole Creek

Tabor Creek

Mary's River

PREVIOUS RESIDENCE
OF FAMILY HEAD

Weber County, Utah:
■ Plain City
◆ North Ogden
● Other Communities

Outside Weber County:
● Utah
○ Non-Utah
   (or unknown)

To Metropolis ↘

Figure 12

Figure 13. Metropolis townsite, early 1913. (Photograph courtesy of the Northeastern Nevada Museum)

Figure 14. Townsite of the Tobar Town Company, May, 1913. (Photograph courtesy of the National Archives)

Figure 15.   Women and child at the Hammond homestead cabin northeast of Metropolis, fall, 1913.   (Photograph courtesy of the Northeastern Nevada Museum)

Figure 16.   Railing sagebrush in Independence Valley, sometime between 1916 and 1919. Paul Striebel of Independence Valley is on the right. The man to the left is Pete Bylund, a farmer from Ruby Valley, Nevada. (Photograph courtesy of the National Archives)

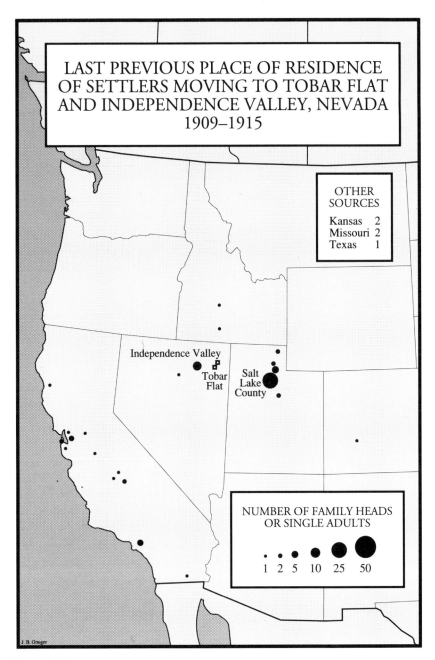

LAST PREVIOUS PLACE OF RESIDENCE
OF SETTLERS MOVING TO TOBAR FLAT
AND INDEPENDENCE VALLEY, NEVADA
1909–1915

OTHER
SOURCES

Kansas 2
Missouri 2
Texas 1

Independence Valley
Tobar
Flat
Salt
Lake
County

NUMBER OF FAMILY HEADS
OR SINGLE ADULTS

1 2 5 10 25 50

J. B. Gouger

Figure 17

land close to friends and relatives who had joined them in the move to Nevada.

Settlement of the Lake Clover plain began in 1904 when a man from Wells occupied a homestead on the northern edge of Tobar Flat, but no further development occurred until the Western Pacific railroad was built through the area in late 1908.[34] At this time several workmen, fed up with their jobs and spotting some likely-looking land near a large but intermittent stream known as "The Slough," filed homestead claims and made plans to return in the spring and try their luck at farming. Among these individuals were George E. Wickizer and Andrew C. Myerhoff, both of German descent, who had earlier moved from the Midwest to Salt Lake City and subsequently found work connected with construction of the Western Pacific. Wickizer had become a Western Union lineman stringing telegraph wires beside the tracks, while Myerhoff, a locomotive engineer, had been engaged to pilot work trains between Utah and the railroad's eastern Nevada construction camps.[35]

In the spring of 1909, Wickizer and Myerhoff, accompanied by three fellow workmen from the railroad, moved onto their claims. Wickizer made especially good progress, and with the help of his brother, who arrived from Kansas in June, he succeeded in clearing seventeen acres and planting fields of grain and alfalfa. Despite losing their first crop to marauding range cattle, the brothers persevered, and by the fall of 1910 they had twenty-six acres under cultivation, evenly divided between rye and Turkey red winter wheat. By this time they owned five milk cows and a hog, and seemed well on their way to establishing a viable farming operation.[36]

The activities of the Wickizers and Myerhoff did not go unnoticed in Salt Lake City, particularly among the city's other German-Americans. To several of these people, development of a new agricultural district near the Western Pacific main line seemed to provide a marvelous business opportunity that could be realized through establishing a town to serve the farming population. Just a few weeks after George E. Wickizer moved onto his homestead, the Tobar Town Company was formed by Max A. Jaensch, a middle-aged, German-born beer salesman who had earlier been involved in townsite speculation in northwestern Utah; William G. Ehlert, a building contractor; and A.J. Weber, an attorney whose downtown offices served as the firm's headquarters. The company was never formally incorporated, and for more than a decade it would exist in name only under the umbrella of Ehlert's contracting firm, Weber's law business, and a hotel operated at the townsite by people hired by Jaensch. Despite its uncertain legal status, the company moved ahead with its plans and soon secured the services of Thomas J. Sweeney, an Irish carpenter known to Ehlert, to supervise construction of its proposed town, which would be located as close as possible to the Western Pacific's Tobar depot.[37]

After trying unsuccessfully for more than a year to purchase a parcel that included the depot, the company concluded that its only option was to build the town on an adjoining piece of public land. The first step in this direction was taken in July, 1911, when Ehlert obtained the rights to an undeveloped quarter-section lying between the depot and the George E. Wickizer homestead, a mile to the south. Two months later, this property was platted as the Tobar townsite, which contained forty-six commercial and residential blocks, with additional land allotted for school grounds and a public park.[38] In the meantime, Thomas J. Sweeney, who was anxious to get started, had moved to Nevada and claimed a homestead southwest of the Wickizer place, about three miles from the depot (Fig. 18). While he awaited instructions from Salt Lake City, Sweeney integrated his activities with those of the other settlers, doing blacksmith work for his neighbors, helping with the construction of sheds and barns, and playing an important role in establishing a community school.[39]

The involvement of the Tobar Town Company and the arrival of Thomas J. Sweeney brought a new dimension to the settlement process. The company made certain that its name appeared in colonization tracts about Nevada and began construction of a combination hotel and store near the northern end of the townsite. Both Jaensch and Sweeney recruited Salt Lake City men to work on the building project and tried to interest them in taking up homesteads on nearby public land. As these events unfolded, the pace of settlement quickened. In April, 1911, the Wells newspaper reported that fifteen prospective farmers from Utah, and a considerable amount of farming equipment, had recently arrived at the Tobar depot. By the end of the year, forty-four homestead entries had been filed in the area, nearly tripling the number on record eighteen months earlier. In four years' time, thanks in part to publicity generated by other promoters who arrived on the scene from California, the number of entries would swell to 115 on Tobar Flat alone and to 141 on the entire Lake Clover plain.[40]

Before the end of 1915, approximately eighty family heads and single adults had occupied land on the bed of Lake Clover. Farmers made up the largest single category, but among the men from Utah they constituted less

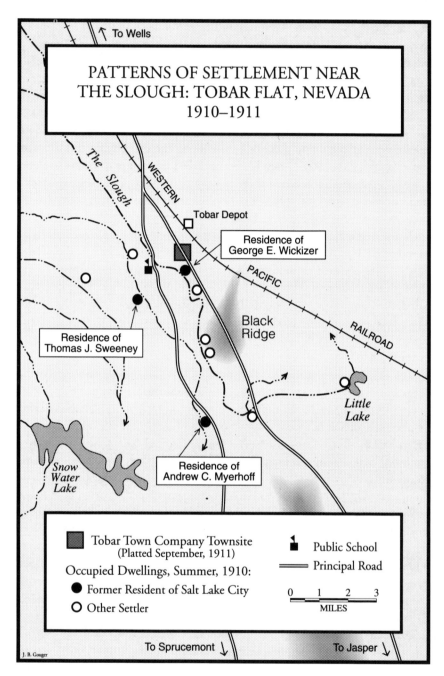

To Wells

PATTERNS OF SETTLEMENT NEAR
THE SLOUGH: TOBAR FLAT, NEVADA
1910–1911

The Slough

WESTERN

Tobar Depot

Residence of
George E. Wickizer

PACIFIC

Black
Ridge

RAILROAD

Residence of
Thomas J. Sweeney

Little
Lake

*Snow
Water
Lake*

Residence of
Andrew C. Myerhoff

Tobar Town Company Townsite
(Platted September, 1911)

Occupied Dwellings, Summer, 1910:

● Former Resident of Salt Lake City

○ Other Settler

■ Public School

Principal Road

0 1 2 3
MILES

J. B. Gouger

To Sprucemont ↓

To Jasper ↓

Figure 18

than ten percent of the total, in contrast to well over half the number at Metropolis and Afton (Table 2). Men with typically blue-collar urban occupations, such as laborers, iron workers, and machinists, were much more common. The handful of women from Utah included two rooming house managers and the estranged wife of a bartender, all former residents of Salt Lake City.[41]

Settlers in this area differed from the people at Metropolis and Afton in more than their occupational backgrounds. Although their ages were similar, barely half of them were married, and of the married couples, about two-thirds were either childless or had only one child, a striking contrast to the colonists in the Metropolis-Afton area, where families with a half-dozen or more children were common. Three-fourths of these individuals were born outside Utah and had been residents of the state for just a few years before moving to Nevada. Most were non-Mormons, principally of German or Irish descent, which further distinguished them from the overwhelmingly Mormon population, largely of English and Scandinavian origin, that had gathered near Metropolis.[42]

About ninety percent of the settlers from Utah, including all of the non-Mormons, came from points within a ten-mile radius of Salt Lake City, with the vast majority living close to the heart of the city. Sixty percent made their homes in a neighborhood of saloons, warehouses, and small factories just west of the downtown area, while most of the others lived on the eastern fringes of the retail area or in the vicinity of the State Fairgrounds.[43] Nearly everyone lived in rented quarters, with most people occupying crowded flats, rooming houses, and second-rate residential hotels. Only three Salt Lake City people—a man who lived with his mother, a middle-aged iron worker, and Thomas J. Sweeney—were not renters. For men and women living in these circumstances, with little prospect of improving the quality of their lives for as long as they remained in the city, the most appealing part of the Back-to-the-Land formula must have been the chance to finally have homes of their own.

It should not be presumed that every blue-collar worker living in a run-down section of Salt Lake City would automatically gravitate to the Nevada desert. In most cases, direct personal contact was necessary to make these individuals aware of opportunities provided by homesteading, to prod them into action, and to point them toward particular destinations. Written statements by the homesteaders, supplemented by circumstantial evidence such

TABLE 2

PREVIOUS OCCUPATIONS OF MEN MOVING TO TOBAR FLAT AND INDEPENDENCE
VALLEY, NEVADA, 1909–1915

	Settlers from Utah	Settlers from Outside Utah	Total
Farmers[a]	3	11	14
General Laborers	4	4	8
Clerks	5	1	6
Railroad Workers	2	3	5
Iron Workers	4	0	4
Carpenters	2	1	3
Machinists	2	1	3
Bartenders	2	0	2
Electricians	1	1	2
Teamsters	1	1	2
Others[b]	6	4	10
Totals	32	27	59

[a]Includes two ranch hands and a farm laborer, all from outside Utah.
[b]Includes a brickmaker, a butcher, a carpet layer, a cesspool cleaner, an embalmer, and a pool
hall operator from Utah and a retired Marine, an oil field worker, a promoter for an oil company, and a street car motorman from outside Utah.

as residence in the same immediate neighborhood or common places of work,
suggests that almost everyone who moved from the Salt Lake City area to the
Lake Clover plain was linked, like the settlers at Metropolis and Afton,
through informal, word-of-mouth networks that led back to a few prominent
individuals, who became catalysts for the entire group.

For example, every person from the Salt Lake City area who homesteaded
on Tobar Flat in 1910 and 1911 was part of a single web of communication
that originated with Max A. Jaensch of the Tobar Town Company and
Thomas J. Sweeney, the company's building contractor. It is unlikely that
any of these individuals would have left the city without assurances from this
pair that public land near the company's property was first-rate, that a viable
town would soon develop near the depot, and that settlers would be able to
support themselves with construction work and other jobs until they made
their homesteads productive.[44]

The network that began with Jaensch and Sweeney also included Edward J. Fitzgerald, who had worked with Sweeney around 1900 and now became one of the group's central figures (Fig. 19). Fitzgerald easily persuaded two of his old friends, William J. Quinn, an embalmer, and Marion Barnes, a railway clerk, to join him in this endeavor. Quinn then brought Fred Kullman, his neighbor, into the group, while Barnes introduced Charles A. Whiting, another railway clerk. Earlier, Fitzgerald had met William W. Tame, an iron worker, and his brother, Wesley, a farmer living on rented land south of the city, and when the movement to Nevada began to take shape, he prevailed upon both of them to come out with the others.

A second part of this network led from Jaensch to F. Eugene Holding, who was operating a pool hall about a hundred yards from a saloon that Jaensch used as his headquarters, and connected these two men with Quinn, who lived right around the corner from the pool hall, and with Kullman, who made his home in a rooming house just a few feet from the saloon. There seems to be little doubt that the four men were acquainted and that one or more of them was responsible for catching the interest of Bertha Lenhart, a rooming house manager who lived about a block from the pool hall. Mrs. Lenhart then drew two of her closest neighbors, Frank Wesley and Amanda L. Kay, into the plan and persuaded her friend, John C. Corbett, a smelter worker, to join her and the others in Nevada. Later, the network would expand still further when Holding succeeded in getting his brother-in-law, Burt Bosley, a butcher who lived just beyond the city limits, involved in the undertaking.[45]

The men and women from Utah were not the first people attracted to Tobar Flat, nor would they be the last. During the first months of settlement, the railroad workers were joined by a handful of individuals from the vicinity of Wells, who occupied homesteads near the lower end of The Slough, not far from where it enters Little Lake.[46] Of much greater significance would be an influx of Californians, beginning in the spring of 1913 and continuing until late 1915. Most of these people originated in Los Angeles or the San Francisco Bay area and were lured to Nevada by the words of California-based promoters, including several with shady backgrounds and questionable motives. The most notorious of the land dealers were the Hoaglin brothers of Los Angeles, whose slogan, "Tobar: Where the Big Red Apple Grows," was a complete fabrication that nonetheless caught the eye of numerous homeseekers.[47]

The Californians would congregate in two parts of the Flat, separated by homesteads already taken by Thomas J. Sweeney and the other colonists from Salt Lake City. Most of the Los Angeles people and a few from the Bay area settled southeast of Tobar on property purchased from the Hoaglins and on public land shown to them by the Hoaglins for the price, it was said, of "$100 a view." The others established homes a half-dozen miles to the west, just beyond the land of the Salt Lake City people.[48] While these events were taking place, a few additional settlers arrived from Nevada and other western states and took land on the Flat's periphery, from a point north of Tobar to the vicinity of Snow Water Lake, and eastward to the lower Slough country.[49] The presence of pioneers from so many different places, with little in the way of common backgrounds or shared values, meant that Tobar Flat would lack the tight social cohesion that characterized Metropolis and Afton, and would also set it apart from the new community taking shape in Independence Valley, where every settler was from Salt Lake City.

The people who moved to Independence Valley in 1914 and 1915 were part of another blue-collar social network that was similar to, and connected with, the network of Salt Lake City residents who had settled on Tobar Flat (Fig. 20). The catalysts here were Paul Striebel, a bartender at the Social Bar, a workingmen's saloon near the southern edge of the city's central business district, and Maude Byrne, the estranged wife of another bartender at the same saloon. After Mrs. Byrne's breakup with her husband, she and Striebel became convinced that they could forge better lives for themselves and the woman's teenaged son in the open spaces and fresh air of Nevada and persuaded a number of saloon patrons to come with them. This group included Celsus P. Heidel, the husband of one of Mrs. Byrne's lifelong friends; Heidel's brother-in-law, Frank T. Koehler; and John A. McRae, a mechanic living five blocks from the saloon.[50]

The other homesteaders also enjoyed close personal contact with at least one other individual who moved to Independence Valley and were probably linked to the saloon-based nucleus of settlers as well. Watson J. Loveless, for example, was an uncle of James P. Farley's wife, while George A. Brown and Arthur W. Brown were brothers, and possibly relatives of Claude C. Brown. There is no evidence to conclusively link any of these people to the patrons of the saloon, but the proximity of this drinking establishment to the rented rooms occupied by Loveless and Claude C. Brown at various times in the early 1900s makes it highly probable that they, too, were integral parts of the same network. Personal ties also connected the three remaining settlers.

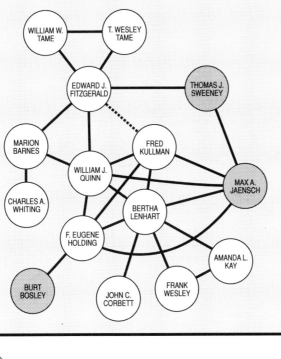

LINKAGES BETWEEN RESIDENTS OF THE SALT LAKE CITY AREA WHO HOMESTEADED ON TOBAR FLAT, NEVADA 1910–1911

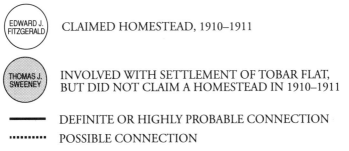

EDWARD J. FITZGERALD — CLAIMED HOMESTEAD, 1910–1911

THOMAS J. SWEENEY — INVOLVED WITH SETTLEMENT OF TOBAR FLAT, BUT DID NOT CLAIM A HOMESTEAD IN 1910–1911

——— DEFINITE OR HIGHLY PROBABLE CONNECTION

·········· POSSIBLE CONNECTION

Figure 19

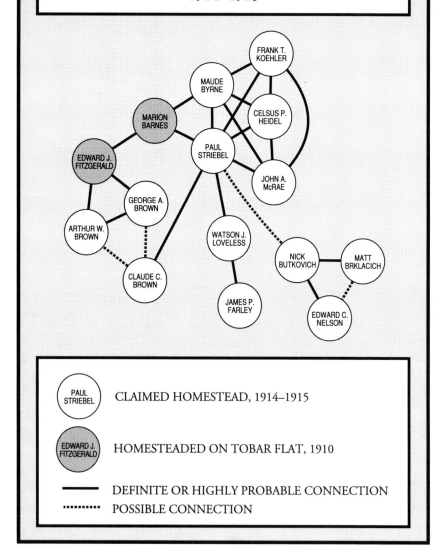

LINKAGES BETWEEN RESIDENTS OF SALT LAKE CITY WHO HOMESTEADED IN INDEPENDENCE VALLEY, NEVADA 1914–1915

PAUL STRIEBEL — CLAIMED HOMESTEAD, 1914–1915

EDWARD J. FITZGERALD — HOMESTEADED ON TOBAR FLAT, 1910

——— DEFINITE OR HIGHLY PROBABLE CONNECTION

••••••••• POSSIBLE CONNECTION

Figure 20

These included Nick Butkovich, a Croatian-born bartender who had been working at a number of west-side saloons; his son-in-law, Matt Brklacich; and Edward C. Nelson, a cesspool cleaner who had formerly lived less than two blocks from a saloon run by Butkovich and who traveled with Butkovich to Nevada, where the two men claimed adjoining parcels of land. Finally, there is no reason to believe that Striebel and Butkovich, bartenders at saloons only five blocks apart, did not know each other, a supposition which, if true, would place the entire body of Independence Valley homesteaders within the same field of personal interconnections.[51]

At least two points of contact existed between the Independence Valley network and the Salt Lake City people now living on Tobar Flat. One of these connected Marion Barnes, the railway clerk, with Striebel and Mrs. Byrne. Before moving to Tobar Flat in 1910, Barnes had lived in the same rooming house that Striebel and the Byrnes occupied, and it is probable that he had conveyed some of his views about the benefits of homesteading to his neighbors. A second link connected Barnes' friend, Edward J. Fitzgerald, with the Browns, whose modest home near the State Fairgrounds was separated from Fitzgerald's house by just three dwellings and two empty lots. When Striebel and Mrs. Byrne began looking for a new place to live in 1914, Barnes and Fitzgerald were still farming on Tobar Flat, sufficient evidence to the people at the saloon, as well as the Browns, that a move to Nevada could prove successful.[52] Additional relationships that may have existed between members of the two networks have been obscured by the passage of time, but two facts remain certain: very few Salt Lake people set out alone for the Nevada desert, and their decisions to participate in this movement can be ultimately traced to direct or indirect connections with Max A. Jaensch and Thomas J. Sweeney of the Tobar Town Company.

The transition from city dweller to homesteader was made with relative ease. Most settlers moving from Utah to Tobar Flat and Independence Valley borrowed small amounts of money, sold or traded household possessions, or spent their few dollars of savings to obtain whatever farming implements, work stock, and seed they would need. For many, start-up expenses were minimal, especially when compared with the expenditures required to establish dry farms on the Great Plains at this time or the costs of getting started several decades earlier in the Middle West.[53] Few of these settlers were planning to adopt standard dry farming procedures, which would require a great deal of cultivation, and in some cases they would not even even plow their fields, choosing instead to plant crops where the soil had been loosened, but not really turned over, during the process of clearing desert shrubs. Thus there was little need for the amount or type of equipment used elsewhere to break prairie sod, cultivate the soil, and prepare additional land for summer fallowing. Indeed, some individuals had no farming implements whatsoever, and traded their labor in return for the help of a neighbor who owned some horses and a cheap plow, probably purchased second-hand. For many, even fencing was a luxury that would have to wait until they had produced a good crop and were on their feet financially.[54] Other settlers were not planning to immediately develop genuine farms and were quite content to do only as much cultivation as necessary to hold their land. For them, homesteads were seen as investments, to be sold for profit at a later date, or as cheap, temporary housing, complete with wells and kitchen gardens, for their families.[55] Under these circumstances, it is easy to understand how poor city people, with few financial resources and very little in the way of equipment or tools, could nonetheless afford to gamble on starting anew in the desert, and have reasonable expectations of success, especially when success could be defined as little more than mere survival.

The move from Salt Lake City to Nevada usually followed one of two routes. People going to Tobar Flat took the Western Pacific to Tobar and fanned out to claims southwest of the Sweeney homestead, which served as sort of a conduit between the depot and the best available land. Most Independence Valley colonists came via the Southern Pacific to Moor siding, east of Wells, and then made their way by desert road to land near the foot of the Pequop Mountains, where, they believed, runoff would provide enough moisture to sustain garden crops and make it possible for some of them to produce small grains.[56]

In the summer of 1915 there were sixty-four occupied dwellings, housing approximately 175 people, on Tobar Flat and in Independence Valley. By this time, some of the first settlers near Tobar had departed, but a solid nucleus of Utah people remained, primarily in an area between the Sweeney place and Snow Water Lake, where fourteen households of settlers originating in Utah lived within a two-mile radius (Fig. 21). Their numbers included six families and single adults from Salt Lake City, two from Salt Lake County, and four additional families from just beyond the city limits in southern Davis County. Three other Utah men, including two from Salt Lake City who had been working in the same downtown department store, made their homes southeast of Black Ridge, separated from the main body of Utah people by one of the two clusters of Californians.

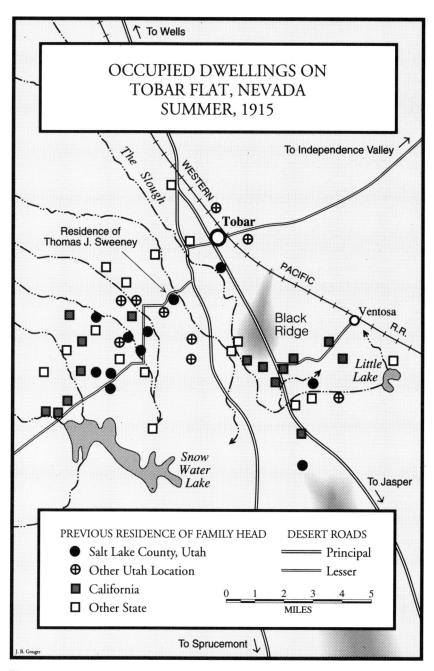

OCCUPIED DWELLINGS ON TOBAR FLAT, NEVADA SUMMER, 1915

To Wells

The Slough

WESTERN

To Independence Valley

Tobar

Residence of Thomas J. Sweeney

PACIFIC

Ventosa

R.R.

Black Ridge

Little Lake

Snow Water Lake

To Jasper

To Sprucemont

PREVIOUS RESIDENCE OF FAMILY HEAD

● Salt Lake County, Utah
⊕ Other Utah Location
▧ California
☐ Other State

DESERT ROADS

══ Principal
── Lesser

0   1   2   3   4   5
MILES

J. B. Gouger

Figure 21

To the northeast, in Independence Valley, were thirteen more households, all occupied by settlers from Salt Lake City (Fig. 22). At the heart of this community were the homes of four of the five individuals who formed the nucleus of the saloon-based social network, each living within a few hundred feet of one another, while the fifth (John A. McRae) lived just a mile to the north. The other homesteaders, with weaker ties to the network's core, fanned out to claims located up to four miles from the heart of the community.[57] Another settler from Salt Lake City, Mrs. LaRue Schulz, was also living in the valley, right across from Maude Byrne's home on former railroad land that now belonged to a speculator from Idaho. The presence of Mrs. Schulz, a former neighbor of Heidel and a friend of the McRaes since 1905, lends further support to the premise that social networks already in existence in Utah were achieving geographical expression on the dry flats of Nevada.[58]

By 1915, the Tobar Flat and Independence Valley settlements bore many outward similarities to the other newly established Nevada farming communities, including those at Metropolis and Afton. Hastily built claim shacks and cabins were giving way to more substantial houses, including a few concrete structures, and barns and sheds, often made of discarded railroad ties, were becoming more common. Fields still showed signs of recent clearing, with clumps of sagebrush standing amidst rows of freshly planted grain, and fencing was far from complete. Section-line roads, in most cases nothing more than narrow trails connecting a few houses, had been laid out in each community.[59] But beneath these superficial features of an emerging rural landscape, the differences were considerable, for unlike Metropolis and Afton, with their rural and small-town Mormon heritage, the social identity of Independence Valley and a substantial part of Tobar Flat was rooted in the predominantly non-Mormon working class neighborhoods of Salt Lake City that supplied a significant share of their residents.

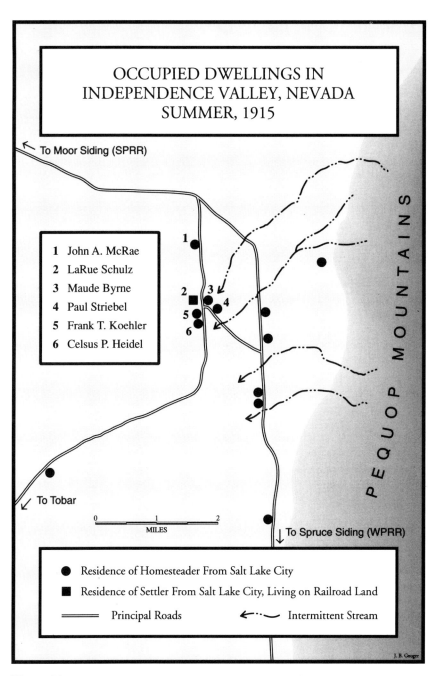

OCCUPIED DWELLINGS IN
INDEPENDENCE VALLEY, NEVADA
SUMMER, 1915

To Moor Siding (SPRR)

1 John A. McRae
2 LaRue Schulz
3 Maude Byrne
4 Paul Striebel
5 Frank T. Koehler
6 Celsus P. Heidel

PEQUOP MOUNTAINS

To Tobar

0   1   2
MILES

To Spruce Siding (WPRR)

● Residence of Homesteader From Salt Lake City
■ Residence of Settler From Salt Lake City, Living on Railroad Land
═══ Principal Roads   ←··⌣ Intermittent Stream

J. B. Gouger

Figure 22

Chapter Three
The Nevada Experience

DECISIONS TO MOVE TO NEVADA AND THE ARRIVAL OF SETTLERS WERE ONLY THE FIRST STEPS in the transformation of the dry valleys near Wells. Land needed to be cleared, fences erected, water obtained, and crops planted. Houses and barns had to be constructed. As the colonists settled in, the structure of community life began to take shape. But these procedures did not occur with uniformity. As the years passed, Metropolis and Afton developed identities which contrasted sharply with those of Tobar Flat and Independence Valley. These, in turn, were the outgrowths of the presence of two different groups of people, influenced by similar yet separate forces, who occupied places with subtle but significant differences in their land and water resources.

PATTERNS OF AGRICULTURE NEAR METROPOLIS

Despite the Pacific Reclamation Company's rapid progress in constructing its dam and canals, farming in the Metropolis area did not go according to plan. The first problems began to develop in late 1911, and worsened in January, 1912, when the U.S. Department of the Interior, which had suspected all along that the company could not possibly irrigate as much land as its advertisements claimed, withdrew 6,300 acres west of the townsite from the project and reprimanded the company for misleading the public about its ability to deliver water to the property it was selling. The unpleasant publicity created by these events, and the company's announcement that it was taking its unsold land off the market, began to arouse suspicions that prospects at Metropolis were perhaps not as bright as the colonists had been led to believe.[1]

Before it could recover from this setback, the company suffered a second, more devastating blow. In April, 1912, just days before water was scheduled to enter the main canal for the first season of irrigating, a Nevada district court issued an injunction forbidding the company to impound or divert all but a tiny fraction of the flow of Bishop Creek until a final judgement had been made about its right to use the remainder of the creek's water. The ruling was made in response to a suit brought by irrigators living near Lovelock, more than two hundred miles down the Humboldt, who feared that diversion of Bishop Creek, and the precedent that this action might set with respect to the Humboldt's other tributaries, posed a serious threat to their own farming activities. Although the company did eventually win the right to use more water, the case dragged on for over three years and caused irreparable damage to the fledgling project.[2]

Within months, what had seemed so promising became a disaster. As soon as it became clear that the water rights issue could not be easily resolved, the company's principal officers, including Harold L. Siegel, severed all ties with the project. By the spring of 1913 the firm was in receivership, both colonization agents had found new jobs in Utah, and the magnificent hotel, opened with great fanfare little more than a year earlier, had closed its doors forever.[3] After passing through the hands of speculators from New York and California, the wreckage was reorganized in 1916 by a mixture of Utah and Massachusetts investors as the Metropolis Land Company, a scaled-down firm whose modest plans went no further than to sustain, as cheaply as possible, the farmers who had remained at Metropolis through the years of litigation. In its first months of existence, the new firm relinquished control of most property held by its predecessors, secured permission to reduce by almost one-half the volume of water that it was obliged to supply to settlers still on the land, and proposed, with the concurrence of state officials, that cultivation of fields below the main canal, originally earmarked for irrigation, be conducted "through the employment of semi-dry farm methods."[4]

Even before these revisions were made official, purchasers of company property had begun to turn their attention to farming without benefit of irrigation. As early as 1913, seventeen of the thirty-two farmers known to be occupying company land were also cultivating dryland homesteads, and of these, at least six, and perhaps as many as ten, were already devoting most of

Figure 23. Turkey red winter wheat grown without irrigation near Metropolis, 1914. (Photograph courtesy of the Northeastern Nevada Museum)

Figure 24. Harvesting grain near Metropolis, c. 1914. (Photograph courtesy of the Northeastern Nevada Museum)

their efforts to land above the canal. Two years later, the number of these fragmented farms had increased to nineteen. By this time, thirteen men were doing most of their farming on their dryland parcels and had relegated their company land to secondary roles, such as grazing and, in a few cases, the production of hay. A good illustration of this trend is the case of John A. Bake, from Hyde Park, who purchased forty acres of supposedly irrigable company land in the spring of 1911, and then, just before Labor Day, claimed a quarter-section homestead two miles above the canal. When it became clear that little or no irrigation water would be made available in 1912, Bake and his family moved up to the homestead, where in 1913 he planted sixty-seven acres in wheat and barley. By 1915 he had a hundred acres in winter wheat and was summer fallowing an additional thirty-six acres in preparation for the next year's planting. Bake's efforts on the homestead far outweighed his activities on his property below the canal, which he used exclusively as grazing land for fewer than a half-dozen horses.[5]

Examination of the pattern of crops planted in 1915 makes it clear that just four years after it was opened for settlement, the Metropolis area had become, out of necessity, a land of dryland grain farms (Fig. 25). North of the canal, Bake and his neighbors had converted several square miles of rolling sagebrush land into a succession of winter wheat fields, creating a landscape not unlike that in parts of Cache Valley, where most of these people had originated.[6] Two farmers in this area had entire quarter-sections under cultivation, while several others had each planted more than fifty acres of dryland grain. West of the townsite, beyond some low, broken hills, another cluster of dry farmers had nearly five hundred acres in grain, while nearby, a newly arrived settler was clearing sagebrush from a half-section of railroad land that would soon be planted in winter wheat.[7]

Dry farming had also become important within the area originally designated for irrigation, especially among those men who did not hold dryland homesteads or had not yet begun to develop them. With the exception of a few settlers living right beside the canal, everyone here had to resort to what the Metropolis Land Company identified as "semi-dry farm methods." This meant that they might occasionally have use of a small amount of irrigation water, but that the volume would be nowhere nearly enough to bring crops to maturity without the application of some dry farming techniques. The county assessor, recognizing that crops grown under these conditions, without benefit of irrigation water or full-fledged moisture conservation measures, would probably not do well, designated them as "fourth class" and

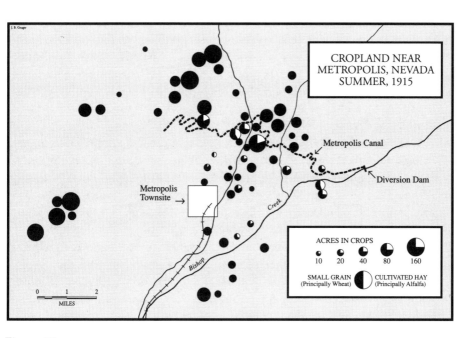

Figure 25

taxed them accordingly. Farmers whose crops fit this category included William T. Hill, from Hyde Park, with an entire forty-acre parcel of company land in fourth-class grain; Fred Calton, from Box Elder County, with thirty acres of fourth-class grain and six acres of equally poor alfalfa; and John Gipson, a former railroad worker from Ogden, whose forty acres, situated less than a half-mile from the canal, were evenly divided between grazing land and a field of fourth-class grain.[8] Despite uncertain yields below the canal and the risks involved in raising crops without a drop of irrigation water above it, Metropolis farmers could agree with an Elko newspaper report that they were "making the best of a bad situation," especially when their grain began to bring prices of $1.50 or more per bushel in Reno and San Francisco. By 1915 they were drawing up plans to build their own flour mill to handle the anticipated increase in wheat production, a sure indicator of the direction in which agriculture seemed to be heading.[9]

Dry farming was also becoming well established at Afton. Here, more than five hundred acres of dryland wheat yielded over ten thousand bushels in 1914, prompting farmers to plant more than a thousand acres in 1915. Afton's most prominent dry farmers were John W. Luckart, the former dairyman from Plain City, who with his sons had 120 acres in winter wheat in 1915; Benjamin F. Blaylock, Jr., formerly a fruit grower in North Ogden, with more than a hundred acres under cultivation, almost entirely in winter wheat; and Alma L. Montgomery, Blaylock's brother-in-law, who had a hundred-acre field of winter wheat. At least seven other dry farmers had planted grain crops, further reinforcing Afton's identity as a promising land where success would be achieved without resorting to irrigation.[10]

Because of the emphasis placed on commercial grain farming, animals played only minor economic roles, except for work purposes or domestic production. Almost every farmer owned a team of work horses, and about two-thirds had milk cows and a small flock of chickens. About half of the families owned a few hogs. But the only settler who could be accurately described as a livestock farmer was a man living a mile southeast of the Metropolis townsite, who owned eleven dairy cows and all but one of the community's seven head of range cattle. Much more representative were farmers like Fred Calton, with a pair of work horses, a milk cow, five hogs, and ten chickens, and John W. Luckart of Afton, who owned two work horses that saw heavy duty in the expansion of his dry farm and those of his neighbors, but no other livestock.[11]

A pressing need for cash forced most men to seek short-term employment away from their farms, even after they had begun to realize some income from their crops of grain. Homestead records and other sources show that over half of the settlers at Metropolis and nearly everyone at Afton were engaged in off-farm work, and it is probable that despite the lack of concrete supporting evidence, the proportion was in fact just as high at the former place as it was at the latter. Some men found employment close to home, on building projects at the townsite, with ranchers' haying crews, and in at least one instance, at a nearby creamery. More frequently, they worked in Utah, usually during the winter months. Most settlers had maintained close contact with their home towns, visiting them whenever possible, and experienced little difficulty finding jobs and places to stay with relatives and former neighbors. There always seemed to be room back in Utah for another temporary laborer or for someone to help out clerking in a store.[12]

The experience of Lytton Y. Mathews, while no doubt extreme, illustrates clearly the need of settlers to support themselves by working away from their farms. In the spring of 1911, at the age of twenty-seven, Mathews claimed a dryland homestead just north of the Metropolis canal, but shortly after establishing residence, his wife died, leaving him with three young children. For the next three years, Mathews' life was a constant struggle to develop his homestead, earn enough money to cover his living expenses, and have enough left over to pay a relative in his home town of Providence thirty-five dollars a month to care for his children. Mathews remained in Providence after his wife's funeral until February, 1912, when he returned to Nevada and found work as a cowboy on a ranch near Metropolis. With the arrival of spring he quit this job, and for the next six months worked with another man breaking forty acres of company land that his brother had purchased, somehow finding time to plant eighteen acres of wheat on his own property as well. Then he left Metropolis and began work as a miner at Bingham, Utah, where he remained until late March, 1913. Mathews spent the next three months on his homestead, interrupted by a week's work at a rodeo in Salt Lake City, and then took a position in Yellowstone National Park until the end of the summer. When this job ended, he moved back to Providence, where he remained until March, 1914, with the exception of one month spent working at the Garfield smelter west of Salt Lake City. From March through November, 1914, he was back in Nevada, where he spent two months on his homestead, held a cowboy job for a month, worked on construction of a schoolhouse in Metropolis for two months, and spent the remainder of his time working for a

Metropolis farmer. Finally, shortly after filing final proof papers on his own homestead, Mathews married the farmer's daughter and returned home to Providence, where he remained for the next three years, except for a quick trip to Metropolis in 1915 to bring back his team. Although he was given legal title to the homestead in 1916, there is no evidence that Mathews ever used his Metropolis land again, and by 1918 he was living in Idaho's Teton Valley, his life once again on an even footing and his Nevada experience gladly behind him.[13]

After 1915, the nature of agriculture in the vicinity of Metropolis and Afton began to change. A series of dry years made unirrigated grain farming unprofitable, a situation that was compounded when wheat prices plummeted after the conclusion of the First World War. To make matters worse, cropland throughout the area was devastated by invasions of jackrabbits and ground squirrels, which caused irreparable damage above and below the canal and destroyed the spirit of men who had invested everything in building up their farms.[14]

These discouraging events were accompanied by developments of a more positive nature, which together helped to alter the area's agricultural patterns. After lengthy negotiations with state and federal officials, the Metropolis Land Company succeeded in working out an agreement, begun in 1916 and finalized in 1923, whereby farmers were assured of receiving a small but certain amount of irrigation water from Bishop Creek. By this arrangement, enough water would be made available to irrigate an area of about 2,700 acres, almost all of it located northeast of the Metropolis townsite. The designated acreage was much smaller than the amount that the Pacific Reclamation Company had originally planned to put under the ditch, but for the farmers it was a satisfactory adjustment, guaranteeing that after a decade of uncertainty, water would be delivered to their fields on a regular basis.[15]

A second positive step was taken in 1917, when John Carlos Lambert, a graduate of Utah State Agricultural College who had been trained as a "dry farm expert," was appointed as Elko County's first extension agent and assigned to Metropolis. Upon his arrival, Lambert encouraged the farmers to continue planting dryland grains and predicted that if they used proper cultivation methods, harvests of thirty bushels of wheat to the acre would become commonplace.[16] But after living in Metropolis for a few years and becoming more familiar with the area's unpredictable climate, he urged them to give up the risky business of dry farming and devote all of their attention to cultivating irrigated land. Calling upon his experiences in Cache Valley, he advised them to diversify their operations, and to place strong emphasis on dairy farming and the production of potatoes.[17] To help achieve these goals, Lambert visited potato growing areas in Idaho to learn more about appropriate cultivation techniques, encouraged suppliers of potato seed to visit Metropolis, and headed a committee of prominent citizens who traveled to Utah to purchase dairy cattle for use by local farmers.[18]

These factors combined to produce a transformation of agricultural life. Some settlers, like Lytton Y. Mathews, who had faced nearly insurmountable odds, gave up and left the area. Those who remained began to concentrate their efforts on land below the canal and to follow Lambert's recommendations about dairying and growing potatoes. One illustration of this dramatic turnaround is the case of Delos W. Hyde, a native of Cache Valley, who in 1915 was living with his family in a three-room frame house on a homestead above the canal, where he had planted forty acres of small grain. By 1922 he had abandoned the homestead and had moved onto a forty-acre piece of irrigated land formerly occupied by a man from Weber County. Here, Hyde had the entire tract planted in alfalfa and kept twenty dairy cows in a stable located a short distance from his solid five-room house.[19] Even John A. Bake, one of the area's most persistent dryland grain farmers, had shifted his emphasis. Bake was still living with his family on their homestead above the canal, but he was no longer farming this property and had given up ownership of the tract of unwanted company land where he had been grazing his horses in 1915. Instead, the family's farming activities in 1922 were concentrated on forty acres of irrigated cropland, located a half-mile from Delos W. Hyde's farm, that Bake's twenty-one-year-old son had obtained from a departing settler.[20]

A survey made by Lambert of farming practices in 1923 reveals the magnitude of agricultural change that had occurred since he arrived in Metropolis. By this time, only thirty-one men were still engaged in farming, compared to approximately sixty just a half-dozen years earlier. Every farmer now owned a herd of commercial dairy cows, ranging in size from eight to thirty-five, with the median number of milking cows standing at nine and the number of heifers at six. The sale of cream, shipped to plants in Elko and Reno, constituted the most important source of income for twenty-one of these men. All but one of the farmers were also growing potatoes, principally for the California market, and they earned, on average, close to three hundred dollars each from this source in 1923. By now, only six farmers were still raising wheat for sale, reflecting Lambert's view that "the growing of grain beyond that needed for home consumption is not profitable, and should be abandoned."[21]

Despite these sensible adjustments, most men still had to work away from their farms to make ends meet. In 1923, thirty of the thirty-one farmers at Metropolis also held off-farm jobs during at least part of the year, and in nine instances the income earned from these nonagricultural sources exceeded that obtained from the sale of cream and potatoes combined. By now, the settlers' ties with Utah had begun to weaken, and most of them found work in northeastern Nevada, often with one of the region's railroads or as hard-rock miners at Spruce Mountain, south of Wells.[22] Still, the need to work away from their farms served as a disappointing reminder that even after a decade of living at Metropolis, these Utah men were not enjoying the kind of success that the Pacific Reclamation Company's promotional campaign had led them to expect.

Pioneer Farming on the Lake Clover Plain

Although settlers in the vicinity of Metropolis had to contend with years of uncertainty about water and were still working away from their farms in the 1920s, their problems were small when compared to the obstacles faced by the Salt Lake City people who had moved to Tobar Flat and Independence Valley. Here, on the desolate plain of Lake Clover, no one could reasonably hope for more than a trickle of water from the mountains, and most people were forced to resort to hit-or-miss methods of moistening their crops from intermittent streams and to waiting for rain. It is not surprising that these transplanted city people seldom advanced beyond the initial stages of pioneer farming or that most of them were able to endure life in the desert for only a few short years.

On Tobar Flat, the adjoining farms of Marion Barnes and Edward J. Fitzgerald were representative of those established by the settlers from Salt Lake City (Fig. 26). Both men had begun by planting potatoes and other garden crops right beside a small meltwater creek whose channel lay just a foot lower than their fields, in the expectation that overflow and seepage during the spring runoff would sustain their crops. Later, they put in crops of grain and alfalfa. By 1914 they had forty acres of cultivated land between them, some of it more than five hundred feet from the creek. But even as

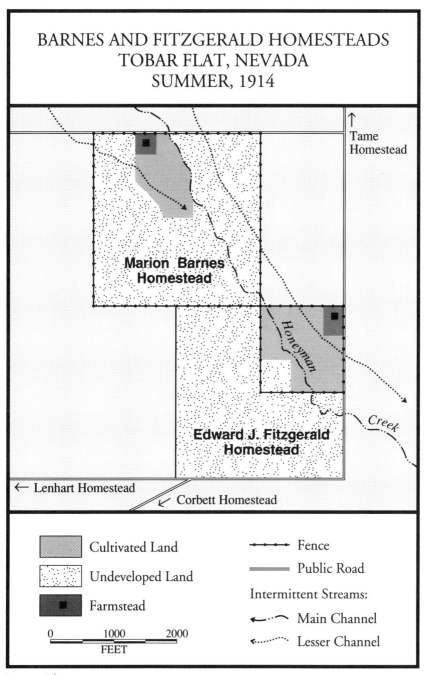

BARNES AND FITZGERALD HOMESTEADS
TOBAR FLAT, NEVADA
SUMMER, 1914

↑ Tame Homestead

Marion Barnes Homestead

Honeyman

Creek

Edward J. Fitzgerald Homestead

← Lenhart Homestead

↙ Corbett Homestead

Cultivated Land

Undeveloped Land

Farmstead

0 1000 2000
FEET

•—•—• Fence

══ Public Road

Intermittent Streams:

←··⌒ Main Channel

←······ Lesser Channel

Figure 26

they edged away from the main channel, the men moved deliberately toward other places where surface flow was likely to be concentrated and laid out their new fields across a pair of even more shallow channels which, they hoped, would deliver a little water in the spring and after midsummer showers.[23] Most of their neighbors adopted similar procedures. A half-mile to the northeast, T. Wesley Tame had thirty acres of potatoes, oats, and alfalfa planted alongside another shallow watercourse, while off to the southwest, Bertha Lenhart and John C. Corbett together had nearly seventy acres in small grain, all of it positioned to receive overflow from several small runoff channels.[24] But even here, in the heart of the Salt Lakers' settlement, no more than ten percent of the total area was under cultivation, telling evidence that farming was not progressing as rapidly on Tobar Flat as in the drylands north of Metropolis.

The experience of William J. Quinn, the former embalmer, demonstrates how difficult it was for the Salt Lake City people to make significant headway. Quinn arrived in Nevada in April, 1911, and moved immediately onto his homestead, located five miles southwest of Tobar. The property, in the words of Quinn and one of his neighbors, was "practically level, with a few little creeks or washes [running] through it," and contained soils that were "dark and heavy in places and light in [other] places, with salt spots," not significantly different from land taken by the other settlers from Salt Lake City. As soon as he had built a shack and dug a shallow well, Quinn grubbed desert shrubs from about ten acres situated near one of the watercourses and planted grain and potatoes. The results were not encouraging. As Quinn later explained, the "crop was a failure because the ground, not having been previously prepared, would not hold the moisture."

Undaunted, Quinn tried again in 1912. With the assistance of a neighbor, who had a team of horses and a good plow, he prepared thirty acres and, once again, put it in grain and potatoes. This time, reported Quinn, the "crop was a failure owing to drought and [jack] rabbits," a somewhat surprising verdict, at least as far as drought was concerned, because the Clover Valley weather station, just eight miles away, had recorded above-average rainfall throughout the entire growing season. The absence of sufficient moisture in Quinn's fields was probably caused by the characteristically spotty nature of the area's precipitation, which could have fallen in the form of heavy downpours near the weather station and inconsequential showers in Quinn's neighborhood, or by the small volume of water delivered by the spring runoff after a relatively dry winter. As for the damage done by rabbits, it is probable that Quinn, like several other Salt Lake City people, had not yet begun to fence his land, and had certainly taken no special measures to keep rabbits and other pests out of his fields. The consequences of this oversight must have been especially galling when Quinn saw that the farmer who helped him plow his fields had raised an excellent crop of potatoes on land enclosed by wire mesh, "rabbit proof" fencing.

Other men might have given up at this point, but Quinn, who was forty-two years and unmarried, with modest personal needs and no better economic prospects in sight, chose to continue. Somehow, he managed to get another seven acres cleared before the spring, 1913, planting season, and when the weather turned warm, he put all thirty-seven acres in wheat and oats. Despite extraordinary June precipitation and above-average rainfall in August at the Clover Valley station and in Wells, his crops did not do well. Quinn reported that the yield of grain was "very light," a result confirmed by a neighbor who added that Quinn's lack of success had occurred "because of drought," once again suggesting that conditions at the weather stations did not always correspond with those out on the Flat.

Heavy snows fell in northeastern Nevada during the winter of 1913–1914, and when spring arrived, the channels crossing Quinn's land and that of the other Salt Lakers filled to overflowing. It appeared that a good year was in store for men and women counting on these little streams to put water in their fields. Indeed, the editor of the Wells newspaper reported after a visit south of town in July, 1914, that the country looked green and promising and that Tobar Flat was "a section where success will come" before long. But at the Quinn place, such optimistic talk had a hollow ring. No additional land had been cleared, and when the harvest season came to an end, it was clear that yields were no better than in the previous year. To make matters worse, Quinn suffered an injury to his eye in October and had to go to Salt Lake City for treatment. He remained in Utah throughout the winter, working to obtain funds to pay his medical bills, and did not return to his homestead until April, 1915. His arrival coincided with a searing drought, and to no one's surprise, the crops that he planted were total failures. Quinn's singular lack of success, year after year, can be blamed on the unfortunate combination of marginal land, insufficient moisture, and an absence of farming experience, all quite normal circumstances for Tobar Flat at this time. What is astonishing is that after so many failures or near-failures, he was still on the land, and that he would remain there, trying to coax something from the reluctant soil, until 1918.[25]

The other Salt Lake City people were no better off. An unusually rich collection of records for the 1913 cropping season shows that within a two-mile radius of Quinn's homestead, four of the six settlers from Salt Lake City harvested nothing at all and that a fifth managed to bring in just a few potatoes. The greatest success, if it can be called that, was recorded by T. Wesley Tame, who harvested fifty bushels of potatoes from a five-acre plot and kept a handful of animals from starving by turning them out to graze in twenty-five acres of grain and alfalfa that was not worth cutting.[26] These pitiful yields were not limited to the men and women from Salt Lake City. Among the people from outside Utah who were trying to farm in this area, the best crops were raised by a former railroad worker, now in his fourth year on the land, who cut five tons of hay from a ten-acre field of spring wheat and dug up enough potatoes to feed his family of five.[27]

Farming practices in Independence Valley bore some similarity to those on Tobar Flat, but they were usually conducted in a more careless manner and brought predictably deplorable results. Several settlers from the saloon, including Maude Byrne, Paul Striebel, and Frank Koehler, clustered around the end of a watercourse that began in the Pequops and disappeared into the desert a short distance beyond their fields. Poorly equipped and hopelessly inexperienced, these people cleared land haphazardly, seldom plowed or cultivated the soil, and in some cases planted crops only once or twice over the course of three or four years. Their single attempt to farm in a more conventional way ended in utter failure when a tractor borrowed from a rancher sank in loose, powdery soil and had to be pulled out by hand. None of these people ordinarily put more than a few acres in crops, and no one enjoyed a bountiful harvest. Their few modest successes stood out dramatically against a succession of numbing defeats. The most noteworthy harvests were two fairly good crops of garden vegetables produced by Mrs. Byrne and some wheat raised by Striebel on a quarter-acre plot, in each case watered by hand from domestic wells. No one produced even a fair dryland crop. The only hint of success achieved without the help of irrigation water occurred when Koehler cut a meager ten pounds of hay per acre from a mixture of wheat, barley, and oats that he had sown in an unplowed tract of land behind his claim shack.[28]

The valley's most ambitious farming endeavor was carried out by James P. Farley and his wife's uncle, Watson J. Loveless, living about two miles southeast of the main body of homesteaders (Fig. 27). The men planted their first fields of grain and alfalfa in 1915 astride two washes coming down from the

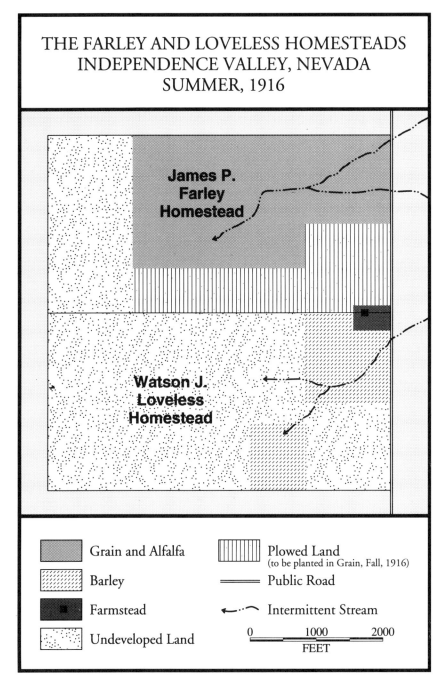

THE FARLEY AND LOVELESS HOMESTEADS
INDEPENDENCE VALLEY, NEVADA
SUMMER, 1916

James P.
Farley
Homestead

Watson J.
Loveless
Homestead

Grain and Alfalfa

Barley

Farmstead

Undeveloped Land

Plowed Land
(to be planted in Grain, Fall, 1916)

Public Road

Intermittent Stream

0   1000   2000
FEET

Figure 27

mountains and did not begin to cultivate land completely beyond reach of runoff until they had exhausted every possibility of putting surface water in their original fields. "We were very enthusiastic for the first two years," recalled Farley, "and broke and cleared about 300 acres." Unfortunately, their first crop died because of drought and the channels' inability to deliver a sufficient amount of water, and their second was struck down by cold weather, leaving the men discouraged and almost penniless. In desperation, they planted eighty acres of fall grain in September, 1916, and then left Nevada to find work, hoping for the best but fearing that the crop would not survive winter conditions at their homesteads' elevation of 5700 feet. When they returned in the spring, wrote Farley, "we . . . found no grain had come up—the severe winter evidently having killed it all." The pair remained in the valley for just a few days, visiting neighbors, selling, trading, or giving away their farming implements and gathering their remaining personal belongings. Before the first of May, 1917, they were gone, never to return. Loveless, by now seventy years old and in failing health, was glad to be rid of the place and wanted nothing more than to return to Salt Lake City and live out his last years in relative comfort, working part-time as a carpenter to support himself. Farley remained hopeful that he and his partner might some day "be able to try our land again and finally make it produce, and pay us back something for our trouble, money, and time," but he admitted in late 1917 that such optimism was unrealistic and that he would probably never see his homestead again.[29]

None of the settlers on Tobar Flat or in Independence Valley placed much emphasis on livestock. Typically, they owned a team of horses, a milk cow, and perhaps a hog, but in many cases they had no animals whatsoever and had to purchase canned milk and meat in town and hire neighbors to help them plant their crops. Even T. Wesley Tame, arguably the best farmer among the Salt Lake City people living on Tobar Flat, and certainly the most diversified, had relatively few animals. In 1915, the year of his greatest farming activity, Tame owned four work horses, two hogs, and a flock of twenty chickens, but by 1917 he had disposed of both hogs and all but one of the horses and was concentrating most of his energy on raising grain, presumably borrowing a neighbor's horse when the need arose.[30]

Several interrelated factors account for the scarcity of livestock in this area. First, most settlers were poor city people who could not afford more than the bare minimum of animals needed to get started. In many cases their inability to raise or purchase feed forced them to dispose of the few animals that they did manage to acquire. John A. McRae, for example, came to Independence Valley from Salt Lake City with a team of horses, a cow, and a calf, but when all of his crops failed, he took the animals back to Utah and in subsequent years hired James P. Farley and others to work his land. McRae's neighbor, Paul Striebel, fared even worse. Striebel arrived in Independence Valley in 1915 with three work horses, but during his first summer on the land two of the horses died and he had to sell the third to obtain money to buy food. Striebel remained in the valley for six more years but was never able to replace the animals and, like McRae, was obliged to hire other men to clear, plow, and plant his land.[31]

Additional economic forces helped to keep the number of animals at a low level. Most Salt Lake City people had come to Nevada hoping to support themselves by raising cash grains, at least until they were well on their feet, and viewed livestock only as sources of power and means of sustenance. To be sure, housewives peddled eggs in Tobar, and occasionally someone sold a hog or a cow, but these were stopgap measures, not the first steps in the development of livestock farms.[32] Furthermore, like the settlers at Metropolis and Afton, these people found that they had to work away from their homesteads for months at a time, making the care of more than a handful of animals a nearly insurmountable burden.

Off-homestead employment became an absolute necessity for almost every settler. More than ninety percent of the Salt Lake City people worked away from their homesteads for three or more months on at least one occasion, with a number of them routinely resuming old jobs in Utah during the winter months. Even a lifelong farmer like T. Wesley Tame was obliged to work as a laborer in Salt Lake City to make ends meet in 1913 and 1914. Others found jobs in Nevada. Edward J. Fitzgerald was employed on one occasion as a miner in the western part of the state and spent several months each year from 1912 through 1916 working at the McGill copper smelter, while George A. Brown of Independence Valley took a job as a section hand with the Western Pacific. Maude Byrne cooked at various ranches in the area for periods of one to four months, and in 1919 she spent five months cooking at a mining camp on Spruce Mountain, thirty miles from her homestead. Several men supplemented their earnings by working for Thomas J. Sweeney whenever he needed help on construction jobs at Tobar, but as the new town's rate of growth slowed, these opportunities began to diminish, making life in Nevada more precarious than ever.[33]

The frequent absences of most settlers meant that neighbors often had to look after their homesteads, care for their livestock, and, occasionally, cultivate their fields. Fortunately, the people from Salt Lake City were no strangers to one another and were usually glad to help out whenever they could. In many cases they combined two or more homesteads into single operational units, with one man doing all of the farming while the other held down a nonagricultural job. In Independence Valley, six of the seven homesteaders who stayed for more than a year generally followed this doubling-up procedure, while on Tobar Flat similar practices were employed by about two-thirds of the settlers from Salt Lake City. If there were no animals to care for, the partner more directly involved with farming might also vacate his claim as soon as crops were in the ground and would not return until fall. In some cases, one or the other paid brief visits to the land in midsummer to inspect their fields and to create the illusion, for the benefit of General Land Office inspectors, that they were living permanently on their homesteads, but they usually fell far short of the government's residence requirements. Several people regularly floated back and forth between their claims and off-homestead jobs, and in some instances neither partner spent more than a week or two each year on the land. This practice was particularly common among the men from the saloon who had taken up homesteads in Independence Valley and among a few late arrivals from Utah who had occupied land on Tobar Flat beyond the original core of settlement. Most of these individuals were not in the habit of breaking the law, but as several of them explained later, they were not very good farmers, either, and in such marginal lands they simply could not afford to put in their crops and wait patiently, hoping for a miracle. In the words of one of the worst offenders, "it was either that or nothing at all. It was impossible to stay there without a way or means of living," and none of the settlers, he felt, could be blamed for bending the rules in order to survive.[34]

Each of the procedures described above gave settlers some flexibility and provided buffers against starvation, but none guaranteed that they would succeed as farmers. Men could locate their fields beside runoff channels and try their best to conserve moisture, but they had no control over the volume of water coming down from the mountains or the amount of precipitation that their crops would receive. Off-homestead employment did not create viable farms from the sagebrush. Combining homesteads into single units would not accomplish anything if crops did not grow. As these facts began to sink in, most settlers on the Lake Clover plain realized that they had made a mistake and that unlike the farmers at Metropolis, who at the very least had a dam for storing irrigation water, a canal, and incomes from their herds of dairy cows, they had few tangible reasons to keep them on the land.

COMMUNITY LIFE

Contrasts between the Metropolis-Afton community and the settlements southeast of Wells went far beyond farmers' relative ability to water their crops or provide feed for their livestock. Residents of the Metropolis area enjoyed the benefits of a tightly knit social organization, especially when compared to the more atomistic nature of society on Tobar Flat and in Independence Valley. Even the two new towns, Metropolis and Tobar, exhibited contrasting social characteristics, in large measure reflections of differences in the nature of their inhabitants and the populations that they served.

The farmers of Metropolis, who understood the benefits that could result from organized group action, became deeply involved in local agricultural affairs. In 1914, for example, several of them traveled to Elko to attend what had been billed as the organizational meeting of a county farmers' society, only to discover that no one from Tobar Flat or any of the other new settlements had chosen to make an appearance. Undeterred, the Metropolis men organized the society themselves, elected their own officials, and began making plans to establish a county-wide farmers' cooperative, which became, through a lack of interest in other places, a Metropolis-based association. During the next few years they held regular meetings at Metropolis, organized livestock shows and several "Potato Days," and scheduled visits by numerous agricultural experts, including members of the University of Nevada agriculture faculty, the director of the university's Agricultural Experiment Station, and Hardy Webster Campbell, the self-proclaimed "Father of Dry Farming." Together, these events provided opportunities, within the context of their own community's life, to devise ways of coping with high desert conditions, to learn about innovative methods of farming, and to develop organized marketing strategies.[35]

A broader, more pervasive type of social organization was supplied by the Mormon church, described by one lifelong resident as "the sustaining backbone of the Metropolis community." Formed in 1912, the Metropolis ward was a vigorous organization that touched almost every aspect of the settlers' lives. In addition to holding regular church services, the ward played the leading role in organizing community social events, hosted conferences of other northeastern Nevada Mormons, and enjoyed regular visits from church leaders based in Utah.[36] Its influence extended well beyond the confines of Metropolis. As soon as there were enough homesteaders living to the north, it established a branch at Afton, with Benjamin F. Blaylock, Jr., serving as presiding elder and superintendent of the Sunday school. Later, when several Metropolis and Afton men went to work in the mines on Spruce Mountain, one of them organized a Sunday School, and reported back to the members at Metropolis about its progress.[37]

The Mormon bishops played critical roles in leading Metropolis through a series of difficult times. When the water crisis continued long after the injunction of 1912, it was Bishop Wilford A. Hyde who represented the beleaguered farmers in negotiations with state officials designed to overcome the impasse. Hyde also traveled to Utah and Idaho in late 1915 to obtain seed grain and hay when these items were in short supply in Nevada.[38] Hyde's successor, Simpson M. Woolf, joined with John Carlos Lambert, the county agent, in the trip to Utah to purchase dairy cattle for the community in the early 1920s. Both Hyde and Woolf provided leadership during the years of rabbit and squirrel infestation, organizing drives, releasing funds for the purchase of supplies to eradicate the pests, and making arrangements for disposal of the carcasses.[39] In the 1930s, Bishop Clifford Jensen, with the help of church officials in Salt Lake City, succeeded in working out an agreement with the Federal Land Bank and other creditors whereby farmers still on the land could finally obtain clear titles to their property.[40] Without the contributions of these men, the Metropolis community would surely have disintegrated much sooner than it did.

The bishops did not limit themselves to these accomplishments. Each one maintained, at least outwardly, a positive attitude toward life in Nevada and encouraged residents to overcome the hardships of pioneering through faith and hard work. Bishop Hyde, for example, reminded the settlers in November, 1912, that "it is God's will that we are here" and urged them to remain in Metropolis and to persevere, a view that was echoed by his principal counselors.[41] Bishop Woolf went a step further. At a time when the area's dryland homesteads were being abandoned, Woolf expressed confidence that "our dry farms will prove to be successful" and actively recruited Mormons from other parts of the state to replace those who were leaving.[42] Even after years of water shortages, rabbit and squirrel invasions, and legal entanglements, this positive outlook persisted. In March, 1937, Bishop Jensen told a church gathering that "we must hang on to our religion to carry us safely through" and added, somewhat illogically, that "this land is a choice land." Jensen's sentiment was matched by that of one of his congregation, who declared at the same meeting that "we have better health and the good things in life by living in a changeable climate," an opinion that other members, despite evidence to the contrary, seemed to share.[43] For these people, the Nevada experience was no longer just an attempt to farm in the desert, but had become more of a spiritual obligation (almost a "mission," in the Mormon sense of the word) to build a lasting community of God.

School activities further unified the community. In 1914, after using makeshift facilities for two years, the citizens of Metropolis built a fine brick schoolhouse, costing $25,000, which became an important focal point for community life. During its first decade of existence, the school offered elementary and high school classes for more than a hundred students annually, and sent a surprisingly large number of its graduates to college. At one point in the early 1920s, five Metropolis young people were attending college, all but one, predictably, in Utah. In addition, the school put on plays and operettas, organized a wide variety of clubs, and sponsored basketball teams for boys and girls. The success of these endeavors was demonstrated in 1923, when a Metropolis youth was awarded first prize at the county fair for his dairy cow, two students won the state debating championship, and the boys' basketball team participated in the state tournament at Reno, winning one game before losing to a team from Fallon. These accomplishments were a source of lasting pride for the community, strengthening its identity as a place where cooperation, dedication, and hard work were important values, and helped make life at Metropolis more than simply a struggle for economic survival.[44]

The town of Metropolis reflected the economic conditions and social organization of the surrounding countryside. During its first year of existence, when it was controlled by the Pacific Reclamation Company, Metropolis contained at least seven retail establishments, including two that were housed in substantial two-story buildings. Nearby were two blacksmith shops, a livery stable, a bank, a doctor's office, and several saloons that catered primarily to construction workers in town and at the dam site.[45] But when the company collapsed, most businesses quickly went out of existence. The saloons were among the first to disappear, for, as Bishop Jensen observed, as soon as Metropolis became a thoroughly Mormon community, "there was no place for them." Nearly all of the remaining businesses closed their doors in late 1913 and 1914. By 1917 only one small store remained in operation, and the "town," only ten miles from Wells' small but active business district, was functioning primarily as a community focal point where farm families congregated for social, religious, and educational functions. The vacant commercial buildings symbolized the area's transformation, in a few short years, from a place of great promise to a community in decline, whose citizens found comfort in the activities of their church and school.[46]

Little of the sense of community that held the citizens of Metropolis and Afton together existed on the Lake Clover plain. Friends and neighbors from Salt Lake City continued to interact with one another, but these people were just one part of a varied settlement mosaic that included urban Californians, newcomers from farms in Kansas and Colorado, and a scattering of Nevada natives. The stabilizing influence of family units was also weaker here than at Metropolis or Afton. Close to half of the adult residents of Tobar Flat and Independence Valley were single people, frequently on the land one day and gone the next, who developed little attachment to place or community. Separation of the population into Mormons, Catholics, and adherents of other faiths did nothing to unify an inherently fragmented society.[47]

Farmers exhibited little interest in organizing activities that might have helped them better their circumstances. When Hardy Webster Campbell visited northeastern Nevada to lecture on dry farming methods, no one invited him to Tobar and few if any men from the Flat bothered to go to Wells to listen to his speech. Most of these city people, unconvinced that meetings and group action could achieve anything, preferred to take the advice of land promoters, who seldom had their best interests at heart, or to follow the examples of the few experienced farmers in their midst, such as T. Wesley Tame.[48] The only evidence of direct involvement in a farmers' organization by anyone from Salt Lake City is a single newspaper item telling of the selection, in 1917, of William J. Quinn, the long-suffering former embalmer, to the board of directors of a farm loan association controlled by promoters and townspeople.[49]

Neither Tobar Flat nor Independence Valley had a church, and the only religious services held in the area were occasional nondenominational Sunday school meetings in a schoolhouse at Tobar. Attendance here was limited to a few local people and some young cowboys from nearby ranches, who seemed to view the activities as a new form of social diversion. Even the handful of Mormons failed to band together. Church records provide no hint of a formal Latter-day Saint presence in this area and show that only one person from Tobar Flat—the wife of a land developer—joined the Metropolis ward.[50] Absence of a church organization is further evidence that a strong sense of community was lacking in these settlements and that their social fabric was markedly different than that of Metropolis and Afton. Certainly, when problems arose, no influential clergyman stood ready to provide direction or to give settlers the strength to carry on.

The school situation led to further fragmentation. Instead of developing a centralized system modeled after that of Metropolis, the citizens of Tobar Flat opted for a number of one-room neighborhood schools, each enrolling about a dozen students in grades one through eight. In 1916, the peak year of their operation, the area was served by five of these schools, scattered across the Flat at intervals of three or four miles. No school was ever established in Independence Valley. The few children who lived in this remote area were taught by their mothers or attended classes in Salt Lake City during the months when their parents were away from their homesteads. Opportunities for a high school education were almost nonexistent. Occasionally someone from Tobar attended the high school in Wells, fifteen miles away, but this was a major undertaking requiring a considerable sacrifice by the student's family. In most cases formal education ended with graduation from one of the little neighborhood schools.[51] Although the schools on Tobar Flat provided the rudiments of an education, the nature of the system, geared to local needs and reflecting local values, did nothing to unify an already loosely knit collection of homesteaders.

The community was divided still further by the existence of two competing townsites near Tobar depot. The Tobar Town Company, controlled by Max A. Jaensch and his Utah partners, was slow to develop its property, and before it had erected more than one or two buildings, it was challenged by the Hoaglin brothers, from Los Angeles, who established their own townsite a quarter-mile to the north. The heated rivalry that developed between the two firms soon led to threats of physical violence, lawsuits, and the defection of Thomas J. Sweeney, the Tobar Town Company's building contractor, to the side of the Californians.[52]

Two dramatic incidents underscored the intensity of this conflict. The first erupted in October, 1914, when one of the Hoaglins caught men hired by Jaensch in the act of moving a building from one townsite to the other and ordered them, at gunpoint, to return the structure to its original location. The men refused and drew their own guns. Bloodshed was averted by Tobar's constable, a transplanted Californian, who arrested all parties except

Hoaglin and took them by train to the county jail in Elko. Upon their release, the men brought suit against the constable, charging that they had been held without a proper warrant. Although the entire case was later dismissed, tension between the groups did not diminish. It surfaced again in March, 1916, when a store owned by the Hoaglins caught fire in the middle of the night and burned to the ground. Arson was suspected, and fingers were pointed at some of the Utah people, but the charred embers yielded no clues, and no arrests were made.[53] If additional serious incidents occurred, they went unreported, but it is certain that hard feelings ran deep in the Tobar area for many years and that the cleavage between the Hoaglins' supporters and those who sided with the Utah men persisted long after the townsite developers had disappeared from Nevada. As late as 1922, the Wells newspaper, which had usually supported the Utah faction, reported with delight that A. B. Hoaglin, creator of the "Big Red Apple" myth, had been jailed in California on charges of selling stock in a nonexistent chain of stores.[54]

Because of its superior trackside location and the more aggressive promotional tactics of its owners, the Hoaglins' townsite became the principal focal point for business activity at Tobar.[55] Their town bore little resemblance to Metropolis.[56] Although both were founded by promoters, Metropolis initially contained a solid nucleus of reputable business establishments, including branches of the most prominent store in Wells, an Elko drug store, and a Salt Lake City farm implement dealership, each managed by responsible people, whereas Tobar projected an entirely different image. Most Tobar proprietors were opportunists who floated in and out of town in search of quick profits, or people down on their luck who came to Nevada to make fresh starts.

Neither of these groups brought much stability to Tobar. The opportunists included one man who transported his store of goods from Kansas to Nevada, pausing only briefly at Tobar before moving on to what seemed like better possibilities in a newly opened homesteading area in Utah. Another was a slick operator, involved in several Tobar enterprises, who later turned his attention to speculating in abandoned mining properties in central Nevada. A third, who left town in 1915 when accused of fraud, surfaced briefly in Carlin, Nevada, then fled to Idaho, and finally turned up in 1917 in southern California. The Hoaglins, operators of a store and saloon as well as their real estate office, were not sterling characters, either, a fact made perfectly clear when one of them was charged by the government with selling public land to unsuspecting homeseekers.[57]

The second category of businessmen included a person who had lost his previous job because of a drinking problem and a man escaping an unhappy marriage in Colorado. One of the most unfortunate of these individuals was Charles H. Heritage, who had operated "The Floradora," a Salt Lake City liquor establishment, in the early 1900s but had since fallen upon hard times. Heritage had drifted to Idaho in search of work and then found his way to Nevada, where he was employed briefly as a miner before opening a saloon at Tobar. He ran the saloon for about a year but died suddenly in January, 1915, at the age of sixty-eight. His saloon business "had not been brisk," observed the Wells newspaper, "and his financial condition was low." The paper added that Heritage's body had been sent back to Salt Lake City, where his wife had remained during his years of wandering.[58]

Businesses changed hands frequently and were often closed for weeks at a time, but for more than three years Tobar usually contained two competing general stores, a drug store, a lumber yard, a livery stable, a blacksmith shop, a large rooming house that passed for a hotel, and another "hotel" that occupied the top floor of a store building. A half-dozen saloons stood open well into the night. At the edge of town was a brothel, run by a Salt Lake City woman brought to Nevada by the Hoaglins, who set her up in business in a structure built to her specifications by the operator of the lumber yard.[59]

When the personalities of its merchants and the nature of the town are taken into consideration, it is not surprising that Tobar's main street saw numerous business-related squabbles and was the scene of a memorable brawl between a storekeeper and the lumber dealer.[60] Most activity, however, was concentrated in places connected with the land business. These included promoters' real estate offices; the drug store, whose proprietor doubled as the General Land Office agent; and the lumber yard, where Southern Pacific property sales were handled. The hotels and saloons, gathering places for homeseekers upon their arrival in town, attracted land sharks of all sorts, including claim jumpers and confidence men intent on stripping a few dollars from the most gullible settlers. Under these circumstances, it was not surprising that when Tobar's first (and only) lawyer hung out his shingle in the spring of 1915, he announced that "land business" was his specialty.[61]

Later, when the Back-to-the-Land movement had subsided and most settlers were gone, Tobar retained its identity as a raw place, unable to shed the coarseness of its formative years. By 1919 it was functioning primarily as a shipping point for ores mined at Spruce Mountain, twenty-five miles to the south, and contained only three places of business—a general store, a saloon, and the lumber yard, whose proprietor continued to peddle railroad land on the side.[62] A half-dozen years later, only the general store remained. By now it was run by a woman whose nose had been eaten away by cancer, leaving two gaping holes where her nostrils had formerly been located. Shunned in the outside world, this unfortunate creature had found refuge at Tobar, where her customers—mostly railroad workers and a few struggling homesteaders—were willing to overlook her grotesque physical features in exchange for the privilege of having a store in their midst.[63]

A person visiting northeastern Nevada in the mid-1920s would have experienced little difficulty distinguishing Tobar from Metropolis. Approaching Tobar, he would have seen an ore loading dock looming beside the tracks, and as he reached the townsite he would pass the remains of the brothel and several saloons before arriving at the general store, where he would undoubtedly encounter the woman with the hideous face, but probably no one else. A trip to Metropolis, in contrast, would have taken the visitor past the schoolhouse and the great hotel, still used occasionally for dances and other special events, and would probably end at the Latter-day Saints Amusement Hall, where, depending on the day and the season, families might be arriving for a church meeting or a basketball game. It would not take long for the visitor to conclude that despite the two towns' Utah roots, the distance between Tobar and Metropolis was measured in considerably more than just miles.

Chapter Four

Collapse

From the very start, settlers in all of the new northeastern Nevada farming communities were plagued by serious problems. Water was constantly in short supply, and invasions of pests, particularly jackrabbits, made consistent crop production almost impossible. It did not take long for disillusionment to set in or for families to conclude that it was time to bring their Nevada experience to an end. For some, departure took place within just months of their arrival. Others withstood adversity a little longer, but by the late 1920s the vast majority had moved away, leaving behind a landscape of empty houses and barns, fallen-down fences, and dusty, uncultivated fields.

Multiple Disasters

Throughout the area, the principal obstacle was a lack of sufficient water for settlers' crops. The first shortage, noted earlier, was caused by the injunction of 1912, which prevented Metropolis farmers from legally using all of the irrigation water that they had anticipated. Although some modifications to the original ruling were made in succeeding years, it was not until 1923 that the issue was finally resolved and farmers were guaranteed access to modest volumes of water. What this meant was that for more than a decade, farmers using land below the Metropolis canal had to make do with uncertain and usually inadequate amounts of water, resort to "semi-dry farm" methods when necessary, and constantly live under the threat that there might come a day when absolutely no water would be available.[1]

73

Shortages of irrigation water at Metropolis were only part of the problem. Dry farmers soon learned that they, too, had made a mistake by relocating in the Nevada desert. After a rainy spring in 1912 and fair years in 1913 and 1914, precipitation in the area plummeted. At Elko, just 6.52 inches fell during all of 1915, while at Metropolis the figure barely exceeded five inches. In contrast to previous years, the summer months were almost bone-dry, with only .07 inches recorded at Elko from June 4 through the end of August. Farmers with fields lying astride small watercourses were no better off than men relying exclusively on rainfall, for unusually low snowfall in the winter of 1914–1915 led to severely diminished runoff in the spring and summer months. Midsummer temperatures approaching one hundred degrees did nothing to relieve a deteriorating situation.[2]

Under these conditions, dryland crop failures were nearly universal, and even among the men who managed to harvest something, yields rarely justified the effort they expended. At Afton, for example, one settler obtained only sixty-three bushels of wheat from forty-seven acres, while his brother, living nearby, harvested just forty-seven bushels from fifty-four acres. Near Tobar, an old rancher remarked that he "wouldn't give ten acres of his irrigated land for a thousand acres of the dry farm country," a sentiment that many others would certainly have echoed.[3]

The next four years were hardly any better. Heavy snowfalls occurred in early 1916, but when the weather turned warm, precipitation fell off to almost nothing. From April through September, Elko received only 1.3 inches of rain, while a shade less than two inches was recorded at Metropolis and Clover Valley. Slight improvements occurred in the spring of 1917 and again in early 1919, but then the bottom completely dropped out. Neither Metropolis nor the Clover Valley station received more than .2 inches of rain from June 1, 1919, through the end of August, while at Elko, no precipitation whatsoever was recorded from May 30 until the last day of September.[4] Once again, crop failures were reported from Afton to Independence Valley, where observations by Utah people that the "crop did not amount to anything owing to [the] dry season" and "crop was a failure, used land as pasture" provided an accurate gauge of conditions on the drylands.[5]

To make matters worse, cold weather struck down some crops that had withstood the drought. The most widespread damage of this sort occurred in 1916, when losses were reported throughout the new farming districts. As James P. Farley of Independence Valley recalled, he and his wife's uncle had justifiably high hopes for a good crop in 1916, "but a freezer came in June and thinned our grain so that we only got a load of hay" from the twenty acres that had escaped complete destruction. Below-freezing weather returned in early September and intensified during the following weeks, making it nearly impossible for some farmers to plant fall grains. No one had worse luck in this respect than Felix P. Toone of Afton. In the fall of 1916, despite three successive crop failures, Toone had sixteen acres ready for planting, but before he was able to obtain seed grain, the ground froze solid, and he had to face yet another year with no income from his farm. Even when summers were warm, remembered Paul Striebel, it was not unheard-of for homesteaders in Independence Valley to have "frost on the Fourth of July."[6]

Farmers recoiling from these weather-related blows were battered still further by onslaughts of jackrabbits. The number of rabbits had been increasing for several years, but until 1915 they had been considered more of a nuisance than a menace. Now, faced with a drought-induced shortage of feed on the rangelands, the rabbits descended on the settlers' property, in some instances consuming the contents of an entire field in the course of a single night. Metropolis and Tobar were identified by authorities as especially hard-hit localities, but in truth the problem existed everywhere. John W. Luckart of Afton reported during a visit to Wells in July, 1915, that he had lost ninety-five percent of his wheat crop to the rabbits and declared that "if you kill one thousand rabbits there will be ten thousand at the funeral." In Independence Valley, Maude Byrne harvested nothing from her half-acre garden because, as she put it, "the rabbits got it all."[7]

Conditions became more desperate in 1916, particularly in the vicinity of Metropolis and Afton, which lay close to the scene of a fierce battle being waged by government forces against the area's coyotes, the principal natural enemies of the rabbits.[8] As the ranks of the coyotes were depleted, rabbit populations exploded, and soon the pests were seen in almost every field, nibbling grain and burrowing into hay stacks. Damage caused by rabbits amounted to almost ten thousand dollars at Metropolis alone, with some farmers reporting losses of several hundred dollars each. A year later, rabbits destroyed three-quarters of Metropolis' dryland wheat crop, which was said (with some exaggeration) to cover ten thousand acres, within a period of just ten days.[9] Meanwhile, ground squirrels had begun to appear in greater numbers than ever before, and by 1917 they were receiving almost as much blame as the rabbits for crop failures at Metropolis and Afton.[10]

Some dry farmers living near Metropolis concluded that it made no sense to put in crops until threats posed by the pests had diminished. One of these

men was William W. Miller, who had failed to harvest anything from ninety
acres planted to wheat and barley in 1915 and again in 1916. "The rabbits
were the cause of so much damage to [his] crops in former years," explained a
friend, that Miller "decided to put . . . his time in 1917 [into] erecting rabbit proof fences, rather than to lose another crop." In 1918, Fred Calton decided to let all of his land lay idle until he could "see what was [to be] done
in regard to exterminating the squirrels." A mile away, Oscar Geertsen, who
had lost his entire wheat crop to rabbits in 1915, to cold weather in 1916,
and to a combination of rabbits and squirrels in 1917, planted nothing in
1918 because he was "sort of discouraged." Geertsen's discouragement was
undoubtedly shared by most other farmers in this beleaguered land. In 1919
they planted only a thousand acres of dryland grain, just a fraction of the
amount under cultivation when the rabbit invasions began.[11]

The effects of drought and the rabbits were aggravated by a loss of manpower when the United States entered the First World War. Several of the
younger settlers, discouraged by persistent crop failures, gladly left their
homesteads to enter military service, and some, recognizing that conditions
had not improved significantly during their absence, never bothered to return. A more subtle effect was a shrinkage of the farm labor pool. Before the
war, settlers who could not work the land themselves had no difficulty finding help, but when this source of labor was absorbed by the armed forces, re-
placements became hard to find. The problem was particularly severe in the
settlements southeast of Wells, which contained fewer people than Metropolis and Afton to begin with, and where the spirit of cooperation was less developed than in the predominantly Mormon communities to the north. Paul
Striebel recalled that "it was pretty nearly impossible" to obtain help in Independence Valley after 1917, while on Tobar Flat a woman who had hired
men to work her land in 1916 and 1917 could find no one to do the job in
1918 and was obliged to let her fields lay idle.[12] Unable to manage by themselves, these and other settlers concluded that it made no sense to continue
trying to operate their farms.

The end of the war brought problems of another sort. As world economic
conditions returned to normal, the price of agricultural products began to
drop. By 1921 the average price received by American farmers for a bushel of
wheat was only ninety-three cents, a marked contrast to 1918 and 1919,
when "two dollar" wheat was the accepted norm. In California, where most
of northeastern Nevada's dwindling grain crop was marketed, wheat brought
just $1.07 a bushel, less than half the amount received in 1918, while in

Utah, the only other destination of even the slightest importance, the price levelled off at seventy-five cents, barely a third of the 1919 amount. For those few farmers around Metropolis and Tobar who were still trying to produce cash grains during these difficult times, it was becoming increasingly evident that their efforts would never pay off.[13]

Personal adversity also diminished settlers' willingness to remain on the land. For some, serious illness or the creeping infirmities of old age made the rigors of homesteading too difficult to bear. Others were devastated by the death of a spouse or other family member. The loss of Bishop Hyde and two of his brothers to typhoid in the winter of 1915–1916 was a terrible blow from which the family never fully recovered, while John W. Luckart found it almost impossible to carry on after the death of a son in 1918. Still others were worn down by the harsh conditions of pioneer life. We can only wonder how many other women shared the disillusionment of thirty-nine-year-old Nancy Hill, who left her husband in February, 1915, after enduring for more than three years with five minor children in a sixteen-by-eighteen foot house on a dryland homestead northeast of Metropolis, prompting her stepson to observe, in a terse understatement, that she was "dissatisfied" with her lot.[14]

COMBATTING ADVERSITY

Although labor shortages, declining prices, and personal tragedies each took their toll, it was persistent crop failure that drove most settlers to the greatest depths of despair. Everyone knew that they could do little or nothing to change the manpower situation or raise prices. But most people believed that if they could find ways to overcome the lack of moisture and get rid of the rabbits, they had a reasonable chance of producing enough paying crops, regardless of the current price of grain, to raise their standard of living by a notch or two. The problem was to select the best plan of action to reach this goal. Methods adopted by the Metropolis-Afton community stood in striking contrast to those tried by settlers on the Lake Clover plain, and reflected the pronounced social differences that separated these two groups of pioneers.

The terrible drought of 1915 brought the question of suitable farming methods to a head. Until this time, only a few dryland settlers were practicing summer fallowing, with the overwhelming majority believing, or hoping, that they could raise crops on a single year's precipitation. The failure of almost all unirrigated crops forced a reassessment of this approach. In the Metropolis-Afton area, thirty-three farmers who had planted winter wheat in the fall of 1914 on continuously cropped land harvested, on average, just a little more than a half-bushel per acre; twenty-six of them failed to produce a single grain. But four other men, farming short distances above the Metropolis canal, had planted their grain in fields that were fallowed in 1914, and when threshing was completed, they reported yields averaging about five bushels per acre. This could not be mistaken for a bountiful harvest, but it was not too far short of the seven to eight bushels generally considered necessary to break even, and was dramatically better than the output of neighbors who had neglected to plant their grain on summer fallowed land.[15]

News of these four settlers' good fortune spread quickly through the Metropolis-Afton community. Speaking at a church meeting in late July, 1915, James H. Allen acknowledged that he had lost most of his crop because of poor farming methods but added that he was not yet ready to give up and predicted that by using techniques applied by their more successful neighbors, he and the other dry farmers would surely "come out all right." This view was echoed by Allen's fellow church members, who declared that by trusting in God and helping one another, they would overcome the effects of drought and, as one of them phrased it, finally make the "sagebrush land blossom as the rose."[16]

The results of this approach became evident within months, as friends and neighbors worked together to put their land in condition to absorb whatever precipitation might occur before the 1916 planting season. In the fall, twenty farmers sowed winter wheat on summer fallowed land, a five-fold increase in just two years (Fig. 28). Within a year, at least four others had joined the ranks of the fallowers.[17] Rapid adoption of this innovation by so many homesteaders, some living more than fifteen miles from farms where the practice of fallowing had begun, is graphic evidence of a community-wide response to adversity, and strong testimony to the effectiveness of a communication web whose focal point was the Mormon church in Metropolis.

Production records for these years are extremely sketchy, but it is certain that in the face of continued drought, wheat planted on land that had been summer fallowed did better than wheat planted on continuously cropped land. In one exceptional case, a Metropolis farmer harvested almost twenty bushels per acre, while several others brought in crops in the six to ten

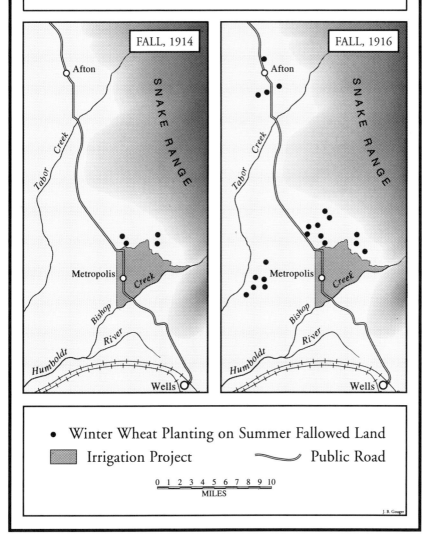

WINTER WHEAT PLANTINGS
ON SUMMER FALLOWED LAND
METROPOLIS AND AFTON, NEVADA
1914 AND 1916

FALL, 1914

FALL, 1916

- Winter Wheat Planting on Summer Fallowed Land
  Irrigation Project   Public Road

0 1 2 3 4 5 6 7 8 9 10
MILES

J. B. Gouger

Figure 28

bushel range. None of the nonfallowers came close to matching these figures.[18] The wisdom of adopting this procedure was made abundantly clear by
Bishop Woolf. Visiting Elko in May, 1919, Woolf declared that "we are very
confident that our dry farms will prove to be successful, as we find that
where the soil is worked along scientific lines, [satisfactory] crops are produced." He added that "the main reason for past failures is that our people
have not followed the proper method in working their soil so as to conserve
the moisture." The bishop's opinion was echoed a month later by the editor
of the Wells newspaper, who reported that the dryland wheat crop at Metropolis had never looked better, particularly on those farms where the soil,
in his opinion, "had been properly handled."[19]

Settlers on Tobar Flat took an entirely different approach. Here, summer
fallowing did not become an important consideration. Only one man (a native of Kansas) had land in fallow when the drought struck, and neither he
nor any of his neighbors followed this procedure in succeeding years.[20] Instead, these struggling homesteaders sought relief in the form of pump irrigation. The process began soon after the crop failure of 1915, when several
people started looking into the possibility of moistening their fields with
ground water pumped to the surface by gasoline engines. Their interest was
probably sparked by the modest success of Joseph H. Parkin, from Woods
Cross, Utah, who had managed to pump enough water from a newly installed well to salvage some of his alfalfa and keep more than two dozen
young fruit trees alive despite almost no precipitation and blistering midsummer heat. They were encouraged by the Hoaglins, always on the lookout
for anything that would make the desolate Flat seem attractive, and by Tobar's lumber dealer, who recognized that he could profit from selling equipment needed to install the pumps and wells. Enthusiasm for pumping grew
rapidly. Within a year, an Elko newspaper observed that in the Tobar area, "it
is now conceded by all who have practiced . . . dry farming methods that it is
necessary to install pumping plants to assist nature [and] produce profitable
crops."[21]

Unfortunately, most settlers found that they could not afford to put in
wells that were deep enough to insure a steady supply of good irrigation
water. Everyone knew that a lens of ground water, sufficient for household
needs, lay just ten to twenty feet beneath Tobar Flat, and it was initially
thought that this source would be adequate for irrigating the parched fields.
But when shallow wells dug in 1916 failed to deliver anything close to the
desired amount, the settlers could see that they would have to go much

deeper, through a zone of impervious material to water located about a hundred feet beneath the surface. For the majority of people, the cost of drilling a deep well, installing a powerful pump, purchasing fuel, and maintaining the equipment was prohibitive, and most plans to combat the drought with ground water had to be dropped.[22] By the summer of 1917, only six wells were in operation, and four others were in various stages of development (Fig. 29). Four wells were owned by former residents of Utah, but just two of these, including Parkin's, were actually in operation. The other working wells belonged to three Californians and a storekeeper from Idaho, all fairly recent arrivals who almost certainly had more financial resources than long-term residents of the Flat.[23] For Salt Lakers such as William J. Quinn, Edward J. Fitzgerald, and Bertha Lenhart, with little to show for their half-dozen years on the land, an irrigation well, and all that went with it, was simply beyond reach.

Although the Idaho man raised one fairly good crop by pumping, the benefits derived from using this method were negligible, and by 1920 all but one of the wells had been abandoned.[24] This brief episode showed, however, that the settlers on Tobar Flat, with little confidence in their ability to raise crops by fine tuning their farming methods, saw their options differently than the farmers of Metropolis and Afton. For them, fighting drought with pump irrigation made more sense than practicing summer fallowing, for it represented a quick fix instead of a measured adjustment, in some ways paralleling decisions made earlier by many of these individuals when they abandoned city life and took a chance on living in the desert.

These contrasts between communities carried over to methods used to combat the rabbits. In the Metropolis area, William W. Miller and a few others built wire mesh fences, but it was the Mormon church that assumed the leading role in the struggle. When rabbit invasions reached crisis proportions in the summer of 1915, Bishop Hyde organized a meeting of farmers to discuss possible solutions, and in October he journeyed to Salt Lake City to obtain the most up-to-date information about eradicating the pests. Through the bishop's efforts, Metropolis and Afton secured the services of a federal agent who taught the farmers how to mix and distribute a strychnine-based poison that would kill the rabbits and how to build pens baited with poisoned hay. Later, Church leaders supervised the assessment and collection of a tax of six cents per acre of cultivated land to continue the poisoning campaign.[25]

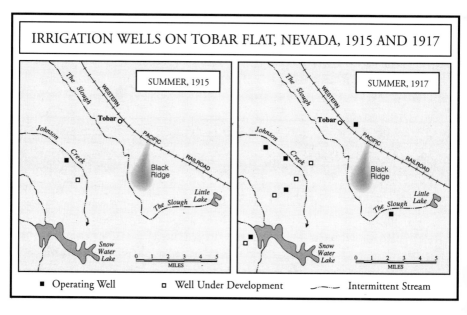

IRRIGATION WELLS ON TOBAR FLAT, NEVADA, 1915 AND 1917

SUMMER, 1915

SUMMER, 1917

■ Operating Well   □ Well Under Development   ⌐⌐⌐ Intermittent Stream

Figure 29

Figure 30. Conclusion of a jackrabbit drive at Metropolis, late 1917. (Photograph courtesy of the Northeastern Nevada Museum)

Figure 31. Remnants of Maude Byrne's sagebrush fence, built in 1919 in Independence Valley. (Photograph by the author)

When poisoning proved ineffective, the church organized a series of rabbit drives, held almost every week during the winter of 1917–1918. Under the direction of Hyde's successor, Bishop Woolf, the citizens drove rabbits from cultivated fields and adjoining tracts of sagebrush land into a large winged corral constructed north of Metropolis, where a group of men clubbed them to death. During the course of the winter, approximately fifteen thousand rabbits were killed in this manner, with carcass counts reaching peaks of 1,200 after one November drive and 1,106 after another in February. Most rabbits were shipped to California, where Woolf found markets among chicken feed manufacturers and, it was rumored, in the fine restaurants of San Francisco, where meat was in short supply because of the First World War. Proceeds from these sources, averaging about twenty cents per rabbit, were used by the church to extend the wings of the corral, to repair damage caused by overexuberant clubbers, and to purchase materials for a twenty-mile-long fence that was supposed to keep the rabbits completely out of Metropolis.[26]

In contrast to these church-sponsored group actions, the war against rabbits on the Lake Clover plain took the form of individual skirmishes. Six Tobar Flat men, including Edward J. Fitzgerald, installed rabbit fencing around their grain fields before the end of 1918, but these barriers, enclosing fewer than three hundred acres scattered across an expanse of several dozen square miles, did nothing to hold back the tide. Most people, unaware of the magnitude of the problem until it was too late and too poor in any case to purchase enough fencing to have an impact, simply left their crops unprotected and hoped for the best. Occasionally one of them shot a rabbit that was careless enough to come within range, or attacked a particularly brazen offender with a club or stick, but these were just individual acts of anger that did little to diminish the number of invaders.[27]

Some people eventually managed to erect rabbit fences around their gardens, but in many cases it was a matter of too little, too late. One of the settlers on Tobar Flat did not get around to enclosing his half-acre garden until he lost everything to rabbits in 1916 and 1917, while in Independence Valley Frank Koehler and his partner, Celsus P. Heidel, made their garden "rabbit proof," to use Heidel's words, only after they had learned the hard way that vegetables left unprotected had no chance against the intruders. But before they could reap any rewards from their labors, drought wiped out the crops that each of these men had planted within their new enclosures.[28]

Even after fences were built, they did not always achieve the desired results. A neighbor recalled years later that rabbits frequently slipped through
Joseph H. Parkin's poorly constructed barrier and that his alfalfa, in particular, was seldom safe. In Independence Valley, Maude Byrne put up a sagebrush fence that succeeded in keeping out most of the rabbits, but it was unable to hold back an army of ground squirrels, which burrowed under the
fence in 1919 and destroyed a small field of grain that someone had planted
for her.[29] Others in the area faced similar dilemmas and found that no matter
what they tried, nothing worked.[30] Without the means, the numbers, or the
social cohesion to mount an effective defense, settlers on the Lake Clover
plain never stood a chance against the pests, and one by one they grudgingly
surrendered to an overwhelming force.

Regardless of what methods were used to combat drought and the rabbits,
it became clear that in the long run, crop failure was almost inevitable. At
Metropolis and Afton, adoption of summer fallowing held down losses, but
it never made dryland grain farming really profitable. A decline in the number of rabbits (brought about as much by disease and severe winters as by the
church-directed campaigns) was more than matched by an upsurge in the
number of ground squirrels, which moved into fields by the thousands.[31] On
the Lake Clover plain, pump irrigation ended almost as soon as it began, and
rabbits and squirrels continued to elude the homesteaders and eat their
crops. When combined with deteriorating economic conditions and personal
hardships, these resounding defeats on the land were often the final chapters
in a succession of disasters that convinced the settlers, once and for all, that it
was time to move on.

Exodus

The enormous problems described above forced hundreds of settlers to
pack up and leave. By 1920 the population of Metropolis precinct (including
Afton) had dropped to just 291, less than one-third of the number of people
on the land just before the water injunction was issued and only about two-
thirds of the area's 1913–1917 population. Only fifty-nine people remained
in all of Tobar precinct (including Independence Valley), where approximately 175 individuals had made their homes in 1915. Five years later almost everyone had left Tobar Flat, Independence Valley, and Afton, and
fewer than two hundred people remained in the vicinity of Metropolis.[32] Al-

though a few departing settlers seem to have simply disappeared, an abundance of records makes it possible to identify the destinations of ninety percent of the Utah people who left Metropolis and Afton between 1913 and 1925 and of an even larger share of those who moved away from the Lake Clover plain.[33]

Approximately sixty percent of the Metropolis-Afton residents who came from Utah returned to their home state, with most of the remainder moving to Idaho, California, or other Nevada localities (Fig. 32). Of those who went back to Utah, two-thirds reestablished residence in their former home towns, and another twenty percent moved to places less than a half-dozen miles from their previous places of residence. The tendency to return home was especially pronounced among those who had lived in Nevada for relatively short periods of time and had never really severed ties with their home communities. Fully seventy percent of the settlers who lived at Metropolis or Afton for five years or less went right back home, whereas there was only about one chance in five that a person who stayed in Nevada for more than five years would return to his former home in Utah.

A significant number of departing settlers, accounting for about one-sixth of the total, moved to predominantly Mormon communities in and around the Snake River valley of southern Idaho, particularly those located only a few dozen miles northeast of Metropolis and Afton. Once again, family ties played important roles in the migration process. Mrs. Deseret C. Storey of Afton, for example, moved in 1920 to Oakley, in Cassia County, to join her son, who had recently relocated there from North Ogden. Before the year ended, Mrs. Storey's cousin, Alma L. Montgomery, had also moved from Afton to Cassia County, where he took up land just a short distance from the Storey place. A short time later, two brothers from Utah who had occupied dryland claims at Afton moved to the outskirts of Rupert, where irrigated land promised them a better future than the bleak Nevada plains.[34] The migration of these people, as well as several others originally from the Plain City-North Ogden area, to southern Idaho suggests the emergence of another dimension of the settlement framework, in which Metropolis and Afton were but small parts in a web of Mormon circulation that was bound together by the ties of church, family, and personal friendship.

Another important destination was Gridley, in California's Sacramento valley. Here, Mormons from Idaho had obtained a foothold in the early 1900s, and as conditions in Nevada deteriorated, the combination of warm weather, a reliable water supply, and an established Latter-day Saint community

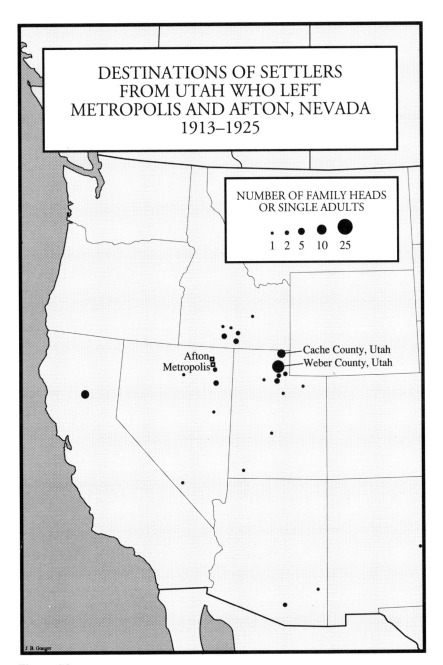

DESTINATIONS OF SETTLERS
FROM UTAH WHO LEFT
METROPOLIS AND AFTON, NEVADA
1913–1925

NUMBER OF FAMILY HEADS
OR SINGLE ADULTS

1 2 5 10 25

Afton
Metropolis

Cache County, Utah
Weber County, Utah

J. B. Googer

Figure 32

provided attractions that some beleaguered Metropolis farmers could no longer resist. William S. Fife and Adna Ferrin, both originally from the Ogden area, were the first to respond to these enticements, but before the end of 1925 four other Metropolis families, including those of Ferrin's brother and his son-in-law, had also moved to Gridley. Correspondence and visits from friends and relatives who had already moved to Gridley soon convinced several others, including a number of Utah-born people who had moved to Metropolis from Star Valley, to relocate in California. Even Bishop Jensen, who had been a pillar of strength for years, finally gave up and moved to Gridley. By the late 1930s the small number of "Metropolis families" living in Gridley had swelled to more than two dozen, a number that would continue to increase as the appeal of California living lured former Metropolis residents who had earlier moved to Idaho or back home to Utah.[35]

A few men, attracted by employment opportunities in the area's mines, smelters, and railroad shops, moved to other Nevada localities. Some remained at these places for several years, but for most of them these moves were merely stopgap measures, and before long they, too, had left Nevada to rejoin family and friends who had gone back home to Utah, or had moved on to southern Idaho or to Gridley. By the mid-1930s, only two of these individuals were still residents of Nevada, a sure sign that the Sagebrush State was no longer seen as a land of promise.[36]

The broad patterns of departure from Tobar Flat and Independence Valley were similar to those exhibited by people leaving Metropolis and Afton (Fig. 33). Utah absorbed about sixty percent of these men and women, with the Salt Lake City area, the principal source of settlers, receiving half of the total number and almost eighty percent of those who went back to Utah. Like the settlers at Metropolis and Afton, the people who stayed in Nevada for the shortest length of time were the ones most likely to return home. In this case, approximately two-thirds of those who had lived on the Lake Clover plain for five years or less went back home, but of the settlers who stayed for more than five years, only one in five returned to his former place of residence, exactly the same ratio that applied to the people from Metropolis and Afton. A small number of Tobar Flat-Independence Valley residents moved to other Nevada communities, but these destinations were usually temporary, and like the settlers from Metropolis and Afton, most of them moved out of the state before many years had passed.

However, significant differences in the specific destinations of departing settlers underscored the basic contrasts between the Tobar Flat-Independence

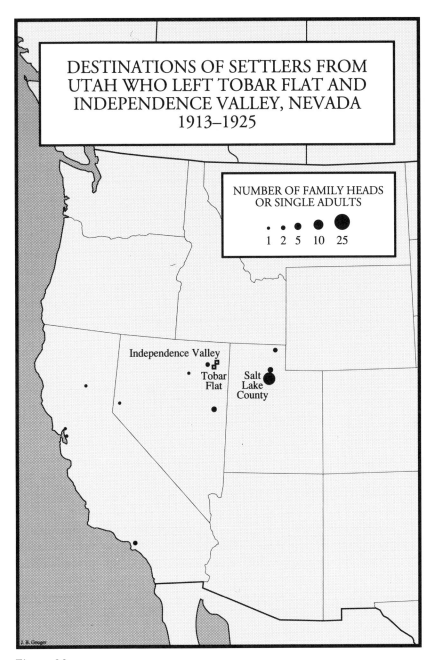

DESTINATIONS OF SETTLERS FROM
UTAH WHO LEFT TOBAR FLAT AND
INDEPENDENCE VALLEY, NEVADA
1913–1925

NUMBER OF FAMILY HEADS
OR SINGLE ADULTS

1   2   5   10   25

Independence Valley

Tobar
Flat

Salt
Lake
County

J. B. Clouser

Figure 33

Valley settlements and the Metropolis-Afton community. No one from the Lake Clover plain moved to Idaho, and of the settlers from Utah who relocated in California, almost every person made his home in an urban setting near Los Angeles or in the San Francisco Bay area. Only one man, George E. Wickizer, moved to the Sacramento valley, and he did not stay very long, for by 1916 he was living in Denver, where he had found work as a Western Union lineman, the same job he held before his homesteading days in Nevada.[37]

Later, several people who had already left the Lake Clover plain drifted out to California, and, once again, they gravitated to urban areas. Thomas J. Sweeney, the Tobar building contractor, moved to Elko in 1916 but then continued on to Oakland, while two others from Tobar Flat ended up in Los Angeles after brief periods of residence in the Salt Lake City area and at Sparks, Nevada. John A. McRae, from Independence Valley, followed a more circuitous route to California. When he finally gave up homesteading in 1919, McRae first went home to Salt Lake City and then moved to New York City, where he was employed as a machinist for close to three years. By 1924 McRae was back in Utah, but a year later he moved again, this time to Los Angeles, not far from the home of James P. Farley, one of his neighbors in Nevada.[38]

One of the best illustrations of this roundabout pattern of migration, beginning in Utah and ending in California, is the case of Mabel Root of Tobar. Mrs. Root, a middle-aged widow, moved to Nevada in 1913 from Colton, Utah, where she and another woman had been operating a rooming house and cafe, on the advice of Max A. Jaensch of the Tobar Town Company, who needed someone to run the company's hotel. When pressure from the Hoaglins forced the hotel out of business in 1914, Mrs. Root decided to try homesteading and moved onto a claim about a mile north of town. With the help of another settler, she cleared forty acres, but she never succeeded in raising a crop and was obliged to work in Utah during the winters of 1915–1916 and 1916–1917 "to make a few dollars to live on." Shortly after completing her residence requirements in June, 1918, Mrs. Root found a job in Salt Lake City, but by 1920 she was living near Corinne, Utah, where she was employed as a cook at a private hunting club. In 1921 she was living on a ranch southeast of Colton, presumably again working as a cook. Then, like so many other people who had once lived near Tobar, Mrs. Root moved to California. Tax records show that she was living in Los Angeles in 1927 and that she had relocated to Carlsbad, thirty miles north of San Diego, in 1928.[39] By this time, seven of the eighteen Utah people who had remained on Tobar Flat long enough to receive title to their homesteads were living in California, with all but one making their homes in southern California.[40]

Two sets of circumstances, one national in scope and the other of an extremely local nature, account for this movement to the cities of California. At the larger scale, these people were just a small part of the huge stream of individuals making their way to California during the 1920s, when two million Americans relocated to the Golden State, primarily to the Los Angeles area. Like Americans everywhere, the migrants from Tobar Flat had lost faith in the Back-to-the-Land movement and now saw better futures for themselves in urban settings. Most of them were attracted by employment opportunities in southern California's expanding economy, and were responding, once again, to the words of promoters and the dream of owning their own homes.[41]

On a more personal level, it is highly probable that the men and women who moved to southern California were also influenced by people who had come to Nevada from the Los Angeles area and were in a position to steer them toward places with which they were already familiar. Although the settlers from Utah and California generally kept to themselves, homestead records and newspaper reports show that some interaction between the groups did occur, and it is probable that information about conditions on the West Coast was passed along during casual conversations over fences or at the post office in Tobar. Overlaps between the social networks of Utah people who moved to southern California and those of southern Californians are unmistakable in the case of Mabel Root and almost certain in that of John C. Corbett and Bertha Lenhart. One of Mrs. Root's best friends in Nevada was Herman H. Schrader, whose cousin, Will Schroeder, had spent several years in Los Angeles before moving to Tobar Flat, while the closest neighbor to Corbett and Mrs. Lenhart in the months before they moved to southern California was a man who had recently arrived from Los Angeles. The effect of these and similar connections on the destinations of departing settlers is made perfectly clear by evidence that every Tobar Flat homesteader from Utah who was living in southern California in the late 1920s had been a friend of someone from Los Angeles when they were residents of Nevada, or had formerly lived less than a mile from a settler from the Los Angeles area. In contrast, no more than a third of the Tobar Flat residents who returned permanently to Utah had personal ties with Californians that can be documented or homes that were located within a mile of a Californian's house.[42] Other evidence that might shed further light on these relationships no longer exists, but there can be little doubt that forces guiding people from the Lake Clover plain to the cities of California were decidedly different from those affecting the migration of former residents of Metropolis and Afton to irrigated farmlands in the Sacramento valley.

Another difference between the two groups, closely related to the first, involved the occupations followed by departing settlers at their new places of residence. Whereas dozens of former Metropolis and Afton people continued farming—in Utah, Idaho, or near Gridley—few people from Tobar Flat and Independence Valley made any further attempts to farm. Insofar as can be determined, no one from Salt Lake County who had lived on the Lake Clover plain ever tried to farm again. F. Eugene Holding, the former pool hall operator, was employed as a structural steel worker and then became a janitor, while his brother-in-law, Burt Bosley, resumed his trade as a butcher for a short time before obtaining a position as a teamster for a wholesale meat dealer. Several other men found work in Utah's smelters. Even T. Wesley Tame, who had almost always been involved in agriculture, gave up at this point and obtained a job with the Utah Power and Light Company in Salt Lake City, where he worked for the rest of his life. The only Utah people who continued farming after living on Tobar Flat were Joseph H. Parkin and another man from Woods Cross who returned to their families' farms after absences of three and four years, respectively.[43] For most people, and certainly for those who came originally from urban settings, a few discouraging years on the sunbaked flats of Nevada were enough to convince them that perhaps, when all options were considered, blue-collar work in the city was not so bad after all.

By 1930 the settlements on Tobar Flat, in Independence Valley, and at Afton were completely abandoned. The citizens of Metropolis held on a little longer, but in the face of drought-induced shortages of irrigation water, renewed rabbit invasions, and uncontrollable increases in the number of ground squirrels, grasshoppers, and Mormon crickets, even the most determined men and women began to cave in. As these adverse conditions went on, year after year, families continued to drift away, usually to Utah, Idaho, or the Gridley area. In 1940, fewer than a hundred people remained in the community. Finally, in the spring of 1949, when the total population had dropped to less than fifty, church authorities disbanded the Metropolis ward, and the school (by now a one-teacher grammar school) was closed forever.[44] These actions, taken less than forty years after settlement began, effectively marked the end of Metropolis as a functioning community and brought the era of agricultural colonization in the northeastern Nevada desert to a dismal conclusion. Writing in April, 1949, the Metropolis Ward clerk wondered "if the Lord is displeased with the efforts that have been put forth in His behalf?"[45] In retrospect, the Lord might well have been pleased with the settlers' efforts, but He was probably still a little disappointed by decisions made decades earlier, when these people and their parents had left their Utah homes to participate in a process that contained so many ingredients for failure.

Chapter Five

A Backward Look

Today, no one lives on Tobar Flat or in Independence Valley. To the north, it is almost impossible to find any evidence on the land that would even hint that the community of Afton once existed. At Metropolis, a half-dozen houses are still occupied, but abandoned fields, dead-end roads, and the forlorn remains of the grand hotel rising from the sagebrush serve as constant reminders that here, too, settlement was generally a failure. Everywhere, there is silence.

For some, scattered ruins and the presence of only a handful of people might imply that settlement of these out-of-the-way places had little lasting significance. But if we take advantage of nearly seventy-five years of hindsight to reflect on the settlers' actions, it is possible to reach conclusions that may well have meaning for the entire Great Basin region. From this vantage point, five important judgements appear to be in order.

First, while the Back-to-the-Land movement was commendable in concept, it is clear that in its application to the Great Basin, it was carried too far. In a land where water is scarce, summers short, and jackrabbits abundant, widespread agricultural settlement was simply not a good idea. It is equally clear that promoters, closely attuned to the pulse of the West, were largely responsible for luring people into this part of the Basin. Without the Pacific Reclamation Company, there would have been no Metropolis, and without Metropolis, the satellite community of Afton would never have come into existence. Most people who settled on Tobar Flat and in Independence Valley were also responding, directly or indirectly, to promotional activities. Perhaps a tiny handful of individuals would have ventured into these dreary places on their own, but the magnitude of the settler invasion,

Figure 34. Foundation of the Hotel Metropolis, including the vault of the Bank of Metropolis, housed in the hotel lobby. (Photograph by the author)

Figure 35. Former residence of Mr. and Mrs. James P. Farley, Independence Valley. (Photograph by the author)

short-lived though it may have been, can only be attributed to the persuasiveness of promoters.

Considering the marginal character of the Great Basin's agricultural resources, these observations should come as no surprise. But this study also brings some heretofore vague impressions about the process of early twentieth-century settlement into sharp focus. It shows that personal linkages played critical roles in this process, that a large share of the people who moved to the dry plains of northeastern Nevada were neighbors, friends, and relatives, and that they established their new homes in close proximity to one another. These circumstances might well have been expected among those who came from small, predominantly Mormon communities, but recognition that linkages were equally well defined among non-Mormons from Salt Lake City sheds new light on the Back-to-the-Land movement in action. It was no accident that the settlers on Tobar Flat were linked to important figures in the Tobar Town Company or that the people who moved to Independence Valley had earlier gathered at a certain saloon on the edge of the city's central business district.

Furthermore, the patterns of migration exhibited by the people who occupied and then abandoned these Nevada valleys demonstrate the existence of two similar but discrete fields of circulation—one for Mormons who settled at Metropolis and Afton and another for non-Mormons who went to Tobar Flat and Independence Valley. A simplified model of these patterns shows that despite sharing common ground in Utah, Nevada, and California, the focal points of each group were different, and the streams rarely overlapped (Fig. 36). Characteristically, Mormon settlers moved from rural and small town settings in Utah to Metropolis and Afton, and when their Nevada experience ended, they chose one of three principal destinations: their home counties in Utah, Latter-day Saint communities in southern Idaho, or a growing Mormon nucleus in the Sacramento valley. Secondary streams of people who initially went to Idaho or back home to Utah generally flowed to destinations already occupied by families who had moved directly from Metropolis and Afton. With very few exceptions, these movements took place within a predominantly Mormon framework in which Metropolis and Afton were simply stopping points, or conduits, between one Latter-day Saint community and another.

Migration streams of the largely non-Mormon population from Utah that occupied the Lake Clover plain paralleled those of the Metropolis-Afton Mormons but flowed to altogether different specific destinations. For these people, the time spent in northeastern Nevada represented a brief rural interlude between more extended periods of residence in Salt Lake City, metropolitan Los Angeles, the San Francisco Bay area, and other urban centers. Admittedly, the number of individuals involved in these particular examples is small, but their movements do seem to show that interactive social and spatial elements were deeply embedded within the migration process. Whether primary or secondary, these streams confirm the existence of discrete networks of people who, at times, lived near each other but seldom interacted and certainly did not move in the same circles.

There is also little doubt that the larger, more cohesive Mormon communities were better equipped to withstand the hardships of desert living than the little settlements of more individualistic homesteaders from non-Mormon backgrounds. Nowhere was pioneering easy, but the social benefits that resulted from the existence of farmers' societies, the activities of a centralized school system, church functions, and perhaps most of all, the leadership of a succession of dedicated bishops, made life somewhat more tolerable at Metropolis and Afton than on Tobar Flat and in Independence Valley. To be sure, the latter settlements contained some good, solid citizens, but without the strength of numbers or a unified front, they could hold out for only a short while against the combined impediments of inadequate amounts of water, too many rabbits, and, for some, a completely foreign way of life. When the new lives that these city people had been trying to build began to crumble, it was only natural that they would return to familiar urban lifestyles, whether in Utah, California, Colorado, or even New York.

On a broader scale, the experiences of these settlers can provide clues to a better understanding of twentieth-century frontier life in other marginal parts of the American West. It seems probable that processes similar to those identified in this study were also operative during the advance of pioneer farmers into the high plateaus of Utah and New Mexico, Washington's Big Bend area, and the West River country of South Dakota, and that they produced equally diverse mosaics of homestead and community that scholars have often overlooked.[1] Environmental, economic, and social forces undoubtedly affected each of these places, just as they had a bearing on patterns developing on other, more distant agricultural frontiers. Together, these forces created significant differences from place to place, with environment playing the most influential role in some instances, economics in others, and social factors in still others.[2] In the case of northeastern Nevada, the social dimen-

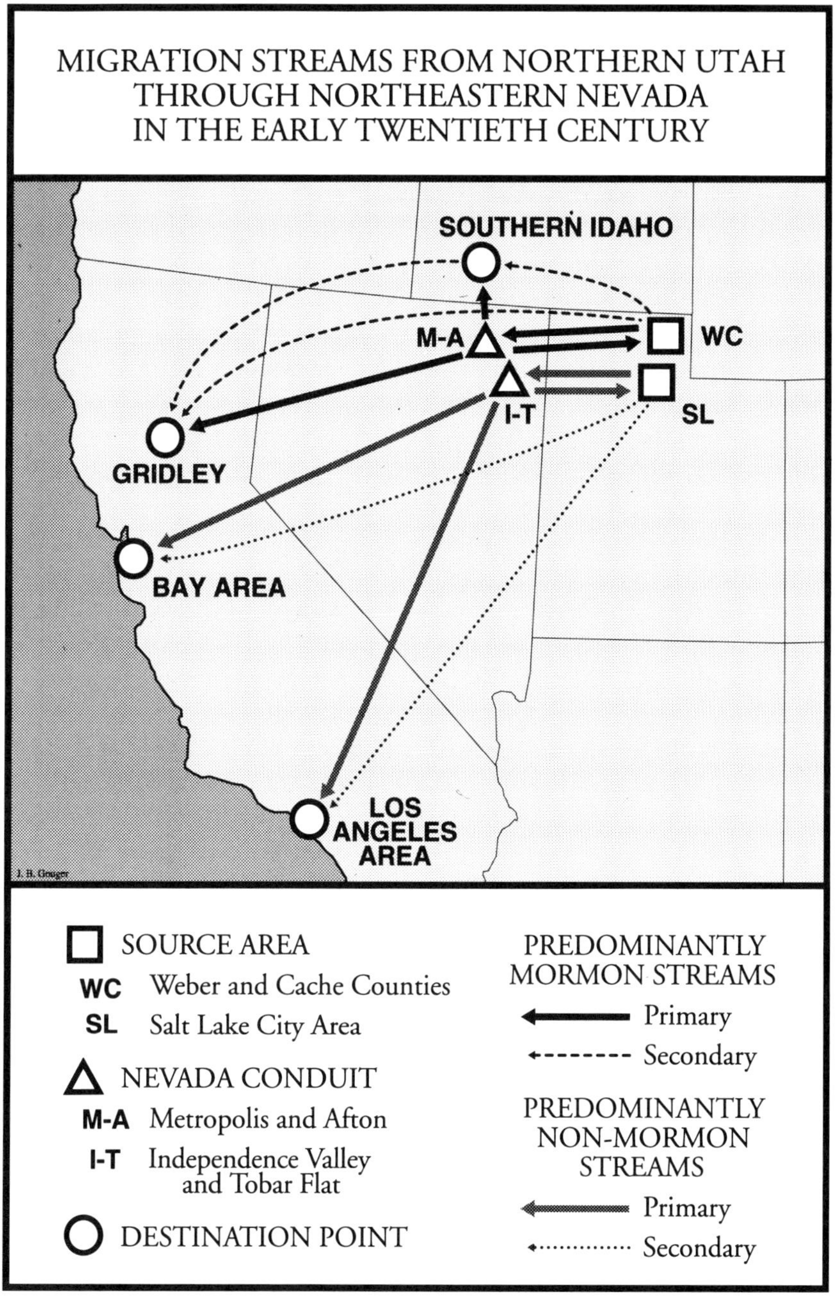

MIGRATION STREAMS FROM NORTHERN UTAH THROUGH NORTHEASTERN NEVADA IN THE EARLY TWENTIETH CENTURY

SOURCE AREA
WC Weber and Cache Counties
SL Salt Lake City Area

△ NEVADA CONDUIT
M-A Metropolis and Afton
I-T Independence Valley and Tobar Flat

○ DESTINATION POINT

PREDOMINANTLY MORMON STREAMS
◀━━━━ Primary
◀------ Secondary

PREDOMINANTLY NON-MORMON STREAMS
◀━━━━ Primary
◀·········· Secondary

Figure 36

sion was most important, particularly when differences are measured by land use practices and the nature of community life.

All settlements under study were affected by northeastern Nevada's harsh environment, especially its unpredictable climate, and by fluctuating economic conditions. Each was established where moisture from surface flow and precipitation was thought to be sufficient to support a mixture of irrigation agriculture and dry farming. Settlers who moved to these places were hoping to better themselves economically through utilization of Nevada farmland, and were encouraged in this direction by sharp rises in the price of wheat. Promoters, too, were seeking to profit while conditions remained promising, and they went to great lengths to attract men and women to supposedly favorable spots in the desert. But because the Metropolis promoters and those at Tobar targeted different groups of people, the communities developed along different lines. When environmental and economic conditions began to change (or, as some would argue, when they returned to normal), settlers perceived these new circumstances through different cultural lenses and responded in ways that were consistent with their social values.

Two examples drawn from shifts in prevailing land use practices illustrate this point. The first took place after the drought of 1915, when the farmers of Metropolis and Afton greatly expanded summer fallowing, whereas the Tobar Flat settlers ignored this possibility and chose instead to try pump irrigation. In the former case, the process followed an orderly, almost predictable course, as information diffused through the fabric of a well-developed, community-wide social network and new methods were implemented cooperatively, with the Mormon church serving as the principal catalyst for communication and action. In the latter instance, it was a case of every settler for himself, with those who could afford pumping plants setting out to install them on an individual basis, while the others did nothing. Homesteaders on Tobar Flat did, of course, enjoy links with neighbors that had existed since before their arrival in Nevada, but their sense of community was never strong enough to overcome built-in cultural obstacles to effective group action.

A second example involves the degree to which livestock-based agriculture was embraced once it became clear that environmental and economic forces were working against profitable production of grain. At Metropolis, the Mormon community cooperated, in both a financial and logistical sense, to effect a changeover from wheat farming to dairy farming. But in the Tobar area, poverty and individualism conspired to keep livestock numbers low, even when the realities of environment and economy seemed to encourage people to stop planting grain and use their land in some other way. In each instance, settlers' values, reinforced by the relative strength of their interpersonal connections, provided frameworks for interpreting environmental and economic pressures, and for making entirely different responses to these pressures.

The nature of community life further illustrated the impact of contrasting values. There is little doubt that the citizens of Metropolis, through their church, school, and farmers' organizations, took a very different approach to living in Nevada than the people of Tobar, where homesteaders congregated in saloons, men visited the brothel, and disagreements between individuals escalated into fights spilling into the streets. Divergent approaches to the jackrabbit problem provide still another yardstick for measuring social distances between the two places. These dissimilarities, in turn, were reflected, directly or indirectly, in patterns evolving on the land.

Critical contrasts between communities, as described and interpreted here, bore remarkable similarities to those identified by Vogt and O'Dea in their 1950s analysis of a Mormon community and a settlement of homesteaders from Texas, located about forty miles apart on the Colorado Plateau of western New Mexico.[3] By focusing on four common issues—supplementary land acquisition, gravelling village streets, construction of high school gymnasiums, and community dances—Vogt and O'Dea demonstrated that cooperative action by the Mormons brought about more positive results than the individualistic approaches taken by the Texans. Their conclusions, based upon intimate familiarity with each community, apply fully to this study, and bear repeating. "For the Mormons," they say, "cooperation has become second nature. It has become part of the institutionalized structure of expectations, reinforced by religious conviction and social control." In contrast, they saw that among the Texas homesteaders, "the strong commitment to an individualistic value-orientation has resulted in a social system in which inter-personal relations are strongly colored by a kind of factionalism and in which persons and groups become related to one another in a competitive, feuding relationship . . . . They interact, but a constant feuding tone permeates the economic, social, and religious structure of the community."[4]

Decades earlier, these same words could have been used to explain why the new farming communities of northeastern Nevada were so readily distinguishable from one another. In the present study, non-Mormons from Utah and California have replaced the Texans, but their values and actions seem to have closely paralleled those of the Texans. Patterns developing on this Nevada frontier were clearly the products of disparate social systems operating side-by-side, one based on the individualism of mainstream American blue-collar society and the other on the traditional Mormon values of community and cooperation, just as they were on the dry plateaus of western New Mexico.

In the final analysis, the evidence presented here suggests that human mosaics created in marginal Western lands were remarkably diverse and that additional research should be undertaken to determine if comparable patterns existed in other parts of this fragmented fringe of settlement. On the one hand, historians and historical geographers must take a closer look at the interplay between the environmental, economic, and social forces that gave birth to patterns of life and livelihood on what was far from a uniform frontier. On the other, we must dig deeply beneath the surface to become more familiar with personalities and value systems that were instrumental in producing significant variations from place to place. Only when pioneer settlement is seen through numerous microscopic studies that reveal the details of ordinary people's lives, and portray distinctions that gave identity to the communities they created, will it be possible to achieve a true understanding of the fundamental nature of these twentieth-century farmers' frontiers.

Notes

The following abbreviations have been used for frequently cited sources and collections:

BLM	U.S. Bureau of Land Management, Reno, Nevada.
ECCH	Elko County Court House, Elko, Nevada.
FARC	Federal Archives and Record Center, San Bruno, California.
GLO	General Land Office
HPA	Homestead Patent Application (General Land Office Serial Patent Files).
LDS	Church of Jesus Christ of Latter-day Saints, Historical Department, Salt Lake City, Utah.
MLC	Metropolis Land Company.
MWHR	Metropolis Ward Historical Record.
NA	National Archives, Washington, D.C.
NDWR	Nevada Division of Water Resources, Carson City, Nevada.
NHS	Nevada Historical Society, Reno, Nevada.
NWS	National Weather Service, Elko, Nevada.
SP	Southern Pacific Land Company, San Francisco, California.
WNRC	Washington National Records Center, Suitland, Maryland.

CHAPTER 1

1. For a review of nineteenth-century agricultural development in the Great Basin, see Leonard J. Arrington, *Great Basin Kingdom: An Economic History of the Latter-day Saints, 1830–1900* (Cambridge: Harvard University Press, 1958), especially 88–95, 148–156, and 215–228, and John M. Townley, *Alfalfa Country: Nevada Land, Water, and Politics in*

the Nineteenth Century (Reno: University of Nevada, Max C. Fleischmann College of Agriculture, 1981), especially 19–40 and 165–182.

2. Paul W. Gates, *History of Public Land Law Development* (Washington: U.S. Government Printing Office, 1968), 647–659; E. Louise Peffer, *The Closing of the Public Domain: Disposal and Reservation Policies, 1900–1950* (Stanford: Stanford University Press, 1951; reprint ed., New York: Arno Press, 1972), 20–21 and 32–42; John M. Townley, *Turn this Water into Gold: The Story of the Newlands Project* (Reno: Nevada Historical Society, 1977), 25–26.

3. Gates, 504–508 and 512–519; Peffer, 144–163. The politics underlying passage of these laws is analyzed in Stanford J. Layton, *To No Privileged Class: The Rationalization of Homesteading and Rural Life in the Early Twentieth-Century American West* (Provo: Brigham Young University, Charles Redd Center for Western Studies, 1988), 21–35 and 61–75.

4. Gates, 503–504; John A. Widstoe and Lewis A. Merrill, *Arid Farming in Utah: First Report of the State Experimental Arid Farms*, Experiment Station Bulletin No. 91 (Logan: The Agricultural College of Utah, 1905), 103–113; John A. Widstoe, "The Present Status of Arid Farming in the Great Basin," *Proceedings of the Trans-Missouri Dry Farming Congress* (Denver: Denver Chamber of Commerce, 1907), 134–141; John A. Widstoe, *Dry-Farming: A System of Agriculture for Countries Under a Low Rainfall* (New York: The Macmillan Co., 1919), 193–204. The development of dry farming east of the Rocky Mountains is described in Mary Wilma M. Hargreaves, *Dry Farming in the Northern Great Plains, 1900–1925* (Cambridge: Harvard University Press, 1957), and Paula M. Nelson, *After the West Was Won: Homesteaders and Town-Builders in Western South Dakota, 1900–1917* (Iowa City: University of Iowa Press, 1986).

5. John Edwin Lamborn, "A History of the Development of Dry-Farming in Utah and Southern Idaho" (M.A. thesis, Utah State University, 1978), 27–73; Carl S. Scofield, *Dry Farming in the Great Basin*, U.S. Department of Agriculture, Bureau of Plant Industry Bulletin No. 103 (Washington: Government Printing Office, 1907); F. D. Farrell, *Dry-Land Grains in the Great Basin*, U.S. Department of Agriculture, Bureau of Plant Industry Circular No. 61 (Washington: Government Printing Office, 1910).

6. Marshall E. Bowen, "Elko County's Dry Farming Experimental Station," *Northeastern Nevada Historical Society Quarterly* 79:2 (Spring 1979): 34–51; George F. Brimlow, *Harney County, Oregon, and its Rangeland* (Portland: Binfords and Mort, 1951; reprint ed., Burns, Oreg.: Harney County Historical Society, 1980), 250–251.

7. David F. Myrick, *Railroads of Nevada and Eastern California*, vol. 1, *The Northern Roads* (Berkeley: Howell-North Books, 1962), and vol. 2, *The Southern Roads* (Berkeley: Howell-North Books, 1963); Don DeNevi, *The Western Pacific* (Seattle: Superior Publishing Co., 1978), 45–60.

8. Examples of the Western Pacific's approach are found in *Western Pacific Mileposts* (San Francisco: Western Pacific Railroad Co., 1953), 28, and throughout brochures titled *Opportunities for Homes and Investments on the Line of Western Pacific*, published from about 1910 through 1915, in the Western Pacific Files, California Historical Society, San Francisco. The role of the railroads in spurring colonization in new lands throughout the country is described in Roy V. Scott, *Railroad Development Programs in the Twentieth Century* (Ames: Iowa State University Press, 1985), 19–35.

9. *Nevada State Herald*, 3 November 1911, 12 April 1912 and 16 May 1913; Transaction Records of the Southern Pacific Land Co. (SP), including notations on the land reclassifica-

tion program, filed at the company's headquarters in San Francisco; the *Salt Lake Tribune*, 1911 to 1917, provides in-depth coverage of promotional activities involving railroad lands in northwestern Utah and northeastern Nevada, much of which is summarized in Marshall E. Bowen, "Promoters and Pioneers: A Perspective on the Settlement Process in the Utah-Nevada Borderlands," *Pioneer America Society Transactions* 15 (1992): 23–31.

10. Layton, 37–39; Hargreaves, 17; Barbara Allen, *Homesteading the High Desert* (Salt Lake City: University of Utah Press, 1987), 121–125; Richard White, "Poor Men on Poor Land: The Back-to-the-Land Movement of the Early Twentieth Century—A Case Study," *Pacific Historical Review* 66 (February 1980): 105–131. The "Back-to-the-Land" movement's place within a broad national context is discussed in William L. Bowers, *The Country Life Movement in America, 1900–1920* (Port Washington, N.Y.: Kennikat Press, 1974), 67–69, and David B. Danbom, *The Resisted Revolution: Urban America and the Industrialization of Agriculture, 1900–1930* (Ames: Iowa State University Press, 1979), 36–39.

11. Allen, 125–126; James H. Shideler, *Farm Crisis, 1919–1923* (Berkeley: University of California Press, 1957), 10–11; L. B. Zapoleon, *Geography of Wheat Prices,* U.S. Department of Agriculture Bulletin No. 594 (Washington: Government Printing Office, 1918), 1–40; C. R. Ball et al., "Wheat Production and Marketing," in *The 1921 Yearbook of Agriculture* (Washington: Government Printing Office, 1922), 139–141.

12. Townley, *Turn this Water*, 31–46, 53–60, and 79.

13. The substantial body of literature in this movement includes Allen, 27–85, Raymond R. Hatton, *High Desert of Central Oregon* (Portland: Binfords and Mort, 1977), 13–42, 52–81, and 94–110, E. R. Jackman and R. A. Long, *The Oregon Desert* (Caldwell, Idaho: Caxton Printers, 1967), 30–64, James Slama Buckles, "The Historical Geography of the Fort Rock Valley, 1900–1941" (M.A. thesis, University of Oregon, 1959), 65–94, and Dale C. Eggleston, "Harney County, Oregon: Some Aspects of Sequent Occupancy and Land Use" (M.A. thesis, University of Oregon, 1970), 85–92. Isaiah Bowman provides a global perspective to these events in *The Pioneer Fringe,* American Geographical Society Special Publication No. 13 (New York: American Geographical Society, 1931), with conditions in the Oregon desert described on pages 93–110.

14. Settlement of irrigated land near Delta is summarized in William R. Jensen, "Canals and Canards: Three Case Studies of Land and Water Speculation in Utah, 1905–1920" (M.S. thesis, Utah State University, 1971), 78–98. Dry farming settlement is discussed in Lamborn, 63–73 and 105–109, and in Carlton Culmsee, "Last Free Land Rush," *Utah Historical Quarterly* 49 (Winter 1981): 26–41. Details on irrigation and dry farming developments are supplied by the *Salt Lake Tribune*, 1911–1917, the *Box Elder News* (Brigham City), 1907–1919, and the *Idaho Enterprise* (Malad), 1909–1915, which covered events in Curlew Valley, Utah, as well as in Idaho. An unusual dimension of the settlement process is analyzed in Robert Alan Goldberg, *Back to the Soil: The Jewish Farmers of Clarion, Utah, and their World* (Salt Lake City: University of Utah Press, 1986).

15. These themes are outlined by Charles S. Peterson in his "Foreword" to Goldberg, *Back to the Soil*, xiii–xx, and in "Imprint of Agricultural Systems on the Utah Landscape," in *The Mormon Role in the Settlement of the West*, ed. Richard H. Jackson (Provo: Brigham Young University Press, 1978), 99–103.

CHAPTER 2

1. *Northeastern Nevada Cooperative Land-Use Study* (Washington: U.S. Department of Agriculture, Soil Conservation Service, 1939), Map 10.
2. *Northeastern Nevada Cooperative Land-Use Study*, Maps 11 and 17; M. D. Mifflin and M. M. Wheat, *Pluvial Lakes and Estimated Pluvial Climates of Nevada*, Nevada Bureau of Mines and Geology Bulletin 94 (Reno: University of Nevada, Mackay School of Mines, 1979), 53 and Plate 1, attached; C. T. Snyder, George Hardman, and F. F. Zdenek, *Pleistocene Lakes in the Great Basin*, Map I-416, Miscellaneous Geologic Investigations (Washington: U.S. Geologic Survey, 1964).
3. John G. Houghton, Clarence M. Sakamoto, and Richard O. Gifford, *Nevada's Weather and Climate*, Nevada Bureau of Mines and Geology Special Publication 2 (Reno: University of Nevada, Mackay School of Mines, 1975), 44–53; U.S. Department of Agriculture, *Climatic Summary of the United States* (Washington: U.S. Government Printing Office, 1932), data for Wells and Metropolis; *Climatological Summary: Wells, Nevada* (Reno: University of Nevada, College of Agriculture, 1970). Items in the Wells newspaper, which kept a close watch on conditions throughout northeastern Nevada, confirm the Metropolis station's reports of heavy snows in the winter of 1913–1914 and almost no precipitation whatsoever during the following winter. *Nevada State Herald,* 16 January 1914, 20 February 1914, 27 February 1914, and 22 January 1915.
4. Houghton, Sakamoto, and Gifford, 29–33; *Climatic Summary*, data for Wells, Metropolis, and Clover Valley; *Climatological Summary*. The Clover Valley station was located near the southwestern edge of Tobar Flat, just a short distance from Snow Water Lake.
5. *Nevada State Herald,* 8 May 1903. For background on the Badt family, see Gertrude N. Badt, "Milton Benjamin Badt," *Northeastern Nevada Historical Society Quarterly* 78:3 (Summer 1978): 90–112, and Chris H. Sheerin, "Three Who Dared: J. Selby Badt, 'Van,' and Ula Vandiver," *Northeastern Nevada Historical Society Quarterly* 80:4 (Fall 1980): 98–113.
6. *Nevada State Herald,* 8 May 1903, 5 May 1905, 26 May 1905, 25 August 1905, 8 September 1905, and 30 July 1909; *Salt Lake Tribune,* 6 August 1911; Elko County tax assessments, 1908–1910, Elko County Court House (ECCH), Elko, Nevada; *Salt Lake City Directory* (Salt Lake City: R. J. Polk and Co., 1908–1910).
7. Frank Nicholas, State Engineer, "Report on Irrigation Project of the Pacific Reclamation Company, Elko County, Nevada," and attached list of Carey Act lands to be set aside, 3 August 1909, supplemented by lists of Carey Act segregations, 21 October 1909 and 28 May 1910, Metropolis Land Co. (MLC) Files, Nevada Historical Society (NHS), Reno; Transaction Records, SP. The company asked for use of 20,706 acres of Carey Act land in July, 1909, but this amount was cut approximately in half during the next ten months.
8. William L. Moran, "A Dam in the Desert: Pat Moran's Last Water Venture," *Utah Historical Quarterly* 50 (Winter 1982): 28–33; William D. Woelz, "Metropolis: Death of a Dream," *Northeastern Nevada Historical Society Quarterly* 3:4 (Spring 1973): 6–8; *Salt Lake Tribune,* 6 August 1911; *Nevada State Herald,* 14 July 1911; *Metropolis Chronicle,* 15 September 19ll; "Map of Metropolis, Nevada," surveyed by J. L. Vandiver, Metropolis Improvement Co., September, 1911, County Recorder's Office, ECCH; Transaction Records, SP.

9. *Nevada State Herald*, 17 February 1911, 14 April 1911, and 29 September 1911; *Metropolis Chronicle*, 15 September 1911 and 15 January 1912; *Salt Lake Tribune*, 6 August 1911; Metropolis Ward Record of Members, Historical Dept., Church of Jesus Christ of Latter-day Saints (LDS), Salt Lake City, Utah.

10. Woelz, 9–10; *Nevada State Herald*, 15 March 1912; *Elko Free Press*, 22 March 1912; author's interview with Mr. Clifford Jensen, former Mormon bishop of Metropolis, Gridley, California, 27 June 1981.

11. *Farm Lands: Metropolis, Nevada* (Salt Lake City: Pacific Reclamation Co., 1911).

12. Woelz, 3–4; *Ogden Standard*, 26 September 1910; *Nevada State Herald*, 4 November 1910 and 29 September 1911. The U.S. Department of Agriculture, in *Climatic Summary*, indicated that annual precipitation at the dam was more than fifty percent higher than at the Metropolis townsite.

13. *Metropolis Chronicle*, 15 September 1911, 1 October 1911, and 25 December 1911.

14. *Salt Lake Tribune*, 28 May 1911, 10 March 1912, and 26 May 1912; *Deseret Evening News*, 2 March 1912; *Ogden Standard*, 17–31 May 1911.

15. *Nevada State Herald*, 24 March 1911, 14 April 1911, 21 April 1911, 9 June 1911, 17 November 1911, 24 November 1911, and 5 January 1912; *Elko Free Press*, 14 April 1911, 21 April 1911, and 26 May 1911; *Metropolis Chronicle*, 1 November 1911; *Ogden Standard*, 27 May 1911.

16. *Metropolis Chronicle*, 15 September 1911, 1 November 1911, and 15 November 1911; Metropolis Ward Record of Members, LDS; General Land Office (GLO) tract books, National Archives, on file at the Washington National Records Center (WNRC), Suitland, Maryland.

17. Moran, 36–38; Metropolis Ward Record of Members, LDS; *Nevada State Herald*, 5 January 1912, 29 March 1912, and 10 May 1912; *Metropolis Chronicle*, 1 May 1912 and 15 May 1912. An injunction issued in the spring of 1912, to be discussed in Chapter Three, severely cut into the Pacific Reclamation Company's right to use Bishop Creek water, drove the company into bankruptcy, and stalled the progress of settlement on company lands.

18. GLO tract books, WNRC; *Nevada State Herald*, 21 November 1913; Jensen interview, 27 June 1981.

19. Woelz, 11; Dale L. Morgan, *The Humboldt: Highroad of the West* (New York: Farrar and Rinehart, 1943), 328; *Nevada State Herald*, 11 October 1912; Metropolis Ward Historical Statistics, LDS.

20. The information in this and succeeding paragraphs is based on a wide variety of sources, principally GLO files, WNRC; Mormon Church historical and genealogical records, LDS; U.S. Census of Population manuscript schedules for 1910; and items in various Utah and Nevada newspapers, which have permitted preparation of a file for each adult known to have settled at Metropolis and Afton between 1911 and 1915. For a review of Mormon migration from Utah in the 1880s, see Richard Sherlock, "Mormon Migration and Settlement after 1875," *Journal of Mormon History* 2 (1975): 53–68, and D. W. Meinig, "The Mormon Culture Region: Strategies and Patterns in the Geography of the American West, 1847–1964," *Annals of the Association of American Geographers* 55 (June 1965): 204–209.

21. The Metropolis Ward Record of Members, supplemented by several family genealogical records, LDS, indicates that 112 of the 116 settlers discussed in this paragraph were Latter-

day Saints. Of six additional settlers whose backgrounds are very obscure, two were probably Mormons and four were not. Other estimates of the proportion of Mormons in the Metropolis-Afton population have been obtained from Marjorie H. Holbrook, *History of Metropolis, Nevada* (Privately printed, 1986), 8, and "Former Townsfolk Remember Metropolis," *Deseret Church News*, 2 September 1989.

22. A few additional single women, including the daughters of William Moroni Ellis and John A. Hall, both in their early twenties, also moved to the Metropolis-Afton area at this time, but lived in their parents' homes.

23. Marie Engh Christensen Storheim, "We Remember Metropolis, Nevada," in Holbrook, 22.

24. *Logan Journal*, 25 November 1909, 7 July 1910, and 11 August, 1910; *Ogden Standard*, 8 and 11 February 1911; Daily Journal of Benjamin F. Blaylock (father of a settler from North Ogden), entries for January–April 1910, and 22 August 1911, LDS.

25. *Utah Gazetteer and Business Directory* (Salt Lake City: R. L. Polk and Co., 1912). A good example of this trend is the case of John W. Luckart, a dairy farmer with ten acres of land at Plain City, who, with two sons, established a dryland grain farm on 480 acres of homestead land at Afton. This view was echoed in an interview on 27 June 1981 with Clifford Jensen, who came to Nevada from Star Valley, Wyoming, with four of his five brothers when it became apparent that they had a better chance of obtaining good-sized tracts of land at Metropolis than at home.

26. Statement attributed to Mr. William Hepworth, who moved to Metropolis with his wife and seven children in 1911, in Woelz, 9–10.

27. For a further discussion of this matter, see Robert E. Bieder, "Kinship as a Factor in Migration," *Journal of Marriage and the Family* 35 (August 1973): 429–439.

28. See note 20, above. A number of Plain City men had become familiar with northeastern Nevada in the early 1900s by working on haying crews that were regularly hired by ranchers in Clover Valley, a short distance south of Wells.

29. See note 20, above, supplemented by Floyd J. Woodfield, ed., *A History of North Ogden: Beginnings to 1985* (Ogden: Empire Printing Co., 1986), 156; statement of Benjamin F. Blaylock, 8 June 1915, Homestead Patent Application (HPA) 497436, WNRC; and North Ogden Ward Historical Record, 3 March 1912, LDS.

30. See note 20, above.

31. See note 20, above, supplemented by *John Anthony Woolf Family Life Histories* (Salt Lake City: John Anthony Woolf Family Organization, 1986), 231–241.

32. GLO tract books and HPAs, WNRC; Elko County tax assessments, 1912–1915, ECCH. Some farm families lived at the townsite in order to be close to church and school, while others made their homes at different times on either company land or homestead property beyond the canal.

33. *Nevada State Herald*, 2 October 1914; *Elko Free Press*, 5 May 1915 and 6 April 1917.

34. Ranchers from nearby Clover Valley had been using Tobar Flat as grazing land since the 1870s, but no one actually lived on the Flat until late 1904, when John C. Munson, a native of Utah who had moved to Nevada around 1900, established residence about two miles west of the future site of Tobar. Edna B. Patterson, Louise A. Ulph, and Victor Goodwin, *Nevada's Northeast Frontier* (Sparks, Nev: Western Printing and Publishing Co., 1969), 428; Munson family genealogical records, LDS; statements of John C. Munson and Eugene Parker, 8 March 1911, HPA 208931, WNRC; *Nevada State Herald*, 9 January 1903, 6 March 1903, 29 January 1904, and 28 July 1905.

35. GLO tract books, WNRC; *Salt Lake City Directory*, 1907–1909; Mary Wickizer Burgess, *The Wickizer Annals* (San Bernadino, Calif.: The Borgo Press, 1983), 7–8; Myerhoff family genealogical records, LDS; author's interviews with Mr. William McDaniel, son of one of the railroad workers who settled on Tobar Flat, McGill, Nevada, 4 July 1979; Mrs. Nettie McQueen, daughter of Andrew C. Myerhoff, Salt Lake City, Utah, 19 July 1982; and Mrs. Opal Troxel, daughter of George E. Wickizer's brother, Theodore, who also settled near The Slough, Wauneta, Nebraska, 20 July 1985.

36. Letter from George E. Wickizer to Louis J. Cohn, Register, U.S. Land Office, Carson City, Nevada, 10 October 1912, and statement of George E. Wickizer, 17 October 1912, HPA 321923, WNRC; Elko County tax assessments, 1909 and 1910, ECCH.

37. *Nevada State Herald*, 11 June 1909 and 24 November 1911; *Salt Lake City Directory*, 1907–1912; *Deseret Evening News*, 1 November 1932; U.S. Census of Population manuscript schedules, 1900 and 1910, National Archives (NA), Washington, D.C.; GLO tract books, WNRC. Jaensch's son-in-law and Theodore F. Wickizer, George's brother, were also involved in development of the townsite and may have invested some of their own money in the project. Ehlert held legal title to the property until 1917, when he sold it to a Salt Lake City promoter, who kept it for a few years and then unloaded it back on Jaensch.

38. U.S. Land Office Affidavit, 3 July 1911, and affidavit sworn by Fred T. McGurrin (one of Weber's law partners) and Theodore Wickizer, 14 November 1911, attached to HPA 401131, WNRC; Map, "Tobar Townsite, Elko County, Nevada," surveyed by H. W. Horne according to a plat prepared by W. G. Ehlert, 11 September 1911, County Recorder's Office, ECCH.

39. Statements of Thomas J. Sweeney, 2 October 1912 and 15 October 1912, HPA 321928, WNRC; *Nevada State Herald*, 11 June 1909, 29 April 1910, and 13 October 1911; McDaniel interview, 4 July 1979; Troxel interview, 20 July 1985.

40. *Nevada State Herald*, 17 February 1911, 7 April 1911, and 24 November 1911; GLO tract books, WNRC; *Opportunities for Homes and Investments* (c. 1913), 10, Western Pacific Files; McDaniel interview, 4 July 1979.

41. The information in this and the succeeding paragraphs has been drawn from files prepared by the author for every family head or single adult who ever settled on the Lake Clover plain. These files utilize records of the General Land Office and the Mormon church, manuscript census schedules, city and county directories, newspaper items, and interviews with children and other relatives of the settlers. From these sources, it is possible to determine the previous occupation of more than eighty percent of the men and women who settled on the Lake Clover plain between 1909 and 1915.

42. Church records indicate that approximately one-third of all Utah people who settled on the Lake Clover plain through 1915 were Mormons, but that Mormons made up no more than a quarter of those who arrived before the end of 1911. Only two settlers from outside Utah (both natives of Utah) were Latter-day Saints.

43. A good portrait of ethnic neighborhoods near the central business district, particularly the area just west of downtown, is provided by John S. McCormick, *The Historic Buildings of Downtown Salt Lake City* (Salt Lake City: Utah Sate Historical Society, 1982), 14–18. Insights to some dimensions of this neighborhood are provided by McCormick in "Red Lights in Zion: Salt Lake City's Stockade, 1908–11," *Utah Historical Quarterly* 50 (Spring 1982): 178–181, and by John Farnsworth Lund, "The Night Before Doomsday,"

Utah Historical Quarterly 51 (Spring 1983): 156–158. Turn-of-the-century Salt Lake City is described in Thomas G. Alexander and James B. Allen, *Mormons and Gentiles: A History of Salt Lake City* (Boulder: Pruett Publishing Co., 1984), 125–161. Details are supplied by *Insurance Maps of Salt Lake City, Utah* (New York: Sanborn Map Co., 1911).

44. *Nevada State Herald*, 25 August 1911, and McDaniel interviews, 4 July 1979 and 9 January 1980.

45. Homesteaders' statements in various HPAs, particularly those of Bertha Lenhart, 18 June 1914, HPA 438434; Edward J. Fitzgerald, 27 October 1914, HPA 472547; Fitzgerald and William Quinn, 17 June 1916, HPA 550934; and Quinn and Marion Barnes, 22 July 1916, HPA 551965, WNRC. *Salt Lake City Directory*, 1908–1911; *Insurance Maps;* U.S. Census schedules, 1910, NA; Holding and Bosley family genealogical records, LDS. Both the pool hall and saloon were located on Second South Street, a short distance from its intersection with West Temple Street.

46. GLO Tract books and statement of George E. Brown, 3 September 1915, HPA 504975, WNRC; author's interviews with Mr. Sim Churchfield, son of one of the early settlers near Little Lake, Elko, Nevada, 26 June 1979 and 16 July 1982; "Some of John and Laura Churchfield's History," papers in possession of Mr. and Mrs. Sim Churchfield, Elko, Nevada.

47. Homesteaders' statements in their HPAs, particularly those of Alma K. Stroud and Everett P. Smith, HPA 668317, and Arthur G. Harley, 23 April 1919, HPA 704575, WNRC; *Los Angeles City Directory* (Los Angeles: Los Angeles City Directory Co., 1911–1914); *San Francisco City Directory* (San Francisco: H. S. Crocker Co., 1912); Jean McElrath, "The Sign Pointed Thirsty 'To Bar,'" *Nevada State Journal*, 21 May 1961; Bowen, "Promoters and Pioneers," 25–27. The Hoaglin Brothers' Investment Company was headed by A. B. Hoaglin, a Los Angeles building contractor, in partnership with his brothers George, a carpenter, and Cornelius, previous occupation unknown.

48. GLO tract books and statement of George S. Hoaglin, 19 July 1918, HPA 668319, WNRC; unpatented homestead files EL 01610, EL 01611, EL 01794, and EL 02208, Bureau of Land Management (BLM), Reno, Nevada; statement of Frank Fouts, 6 March 1918, Contest No. 177, U.S. Land Office, Elko, Nevada, on file at the Federal Archives and Record Center (FARC), San Bruno, California; Transaction Records, SP; *Nevada State Herald*, 25 April 1913; McElrath.

49. Statements of Clarence M. Beals, 1 February 1916, HPA 527244; Henry E. Boehme, 25 July 1916, HPA 555012; James Bissell, 7 April 1919, HPA 703534; William J. Blackwell, 12 April 1919, HPA 704573; and Donna B. Green, 12 April 1919, HPA 704576, WNRC. Unpatented homestead files EL 01488 and 01792, BLM.

50. The Social Bar was located in the 500 block of South State Street. The role of saloons as focal points for ethnic neighborhoods in the urban West around the turn of the century is discussed in Thomas J. Noel, *The City and the Saloon: Denver, 1858–1916* (Lincoln: University of Nebraska Press, 1982), 53–66, and Joseph Stipanovich, *The South Slavs in Utah: A Social History* (San Francisco: R and E Research Associates, 1975), 77–78.

51. Affidavit filed by Maude Byrne, 24 August 1914, HPA 777013; letter from Watson J. Loveless to Clay Tallman, U.S. Land Commissioner, 14 August 1917, HPA 623102; letter from N. F. Waddell, Special Agent, GLO, to Commissioner, GLO, 9 March 1922, and testimony of Paul Striebel and Maude (Byrne) Sloan, 25 November 1922, in *U.S. v. McRae*, attached to HPA 929616, WNRC. U.S. Census schedules, 1900 and 1910, NA;

Salt Lake City Directory, 1906–1914; *Deseret Evening News*, 18 August 1953 and 17 February 1970; *Salt Lake Tribune*, 4 October 1953.

52. U.S. Census schedules, 1910, NA; *Salt Lake City Directory*, 1909–1914; *Insurance Maps;* statements of Marion Barnes, 17 June 1916, HPA 550934, and Edward J. Fitzgerald, 25 July 1916, HPA 551965, WNRC.

53. The situation on the Great Plains is summarized in Hargreaves, 519–520. For the Middle West, see Allan G. Bogue's observations in *Money at Interest: The Farm Mortgage on the Middle Border* (Ithaca: Cornell University Press, 1955), 2–4, and *From Prairie to Corn Belt: Farming on the Illinois and Iowa Prairies in the Nineteenth Century* (Chicago: University of Chicago Press, 1963), 67–71. It is thought that the Tobar Town Company may have underwritten part of some settlers' start-up expenses in return for work on the townsite, but it is doubtful if this condition applied to all of the homesteaders who moved from Salt Lake City to Tobar Flat. McDaniel interview, 9 January 1980.

54. Testimony of Paul Striebel and Pete Bylund, 25 November 1922, in *U.S. v. McRae*, attached to HPA 929616, and homesteaders' statements in their HPAs, particularly those of Bertha Lenhart, 18 June 1914, HPA 438433, and Maude (Byrne) Sloan, 3 March 1920, HPA 777013, WNRC; McDaniel interview, 9 January 1980, and author's interview with Eugene Pengelly, a former mayor of Wells and personal friend of several settler families on Tobar Flat and in Independence Valley, Wells, Nevada, 22 June 1982.

55. Sales and proposed sales of partially developed homestead property on Tobar Flat are recorded in the *Salt Lake Tribune*, 26 May 1912 and 18 May 1913, and in the statement of Arthur G. Harley, 23 April 1919, HPA 704575, WNRC. The practice of many northeastern Nevada homesteaders, including some in Independence Valley, to establish homes for their families without making bonafide attempts to farm is described in Marshall Bowen, "The Desert Homestead as a Non-Farm Residence," *Nevada Historical Society Quarterly* 31 (Fall 1988): 198–211.

56. *Nevada State Herald*, 7 April 1911 and 25 August 1911; GLO tract books; letter from James P. Farley to Clay Tallman, U.S. Land Commissioner, 11 August 1917, HPA 623101, and testimony of John A, McRae, 25 November 1922, in *U.S. v. McRae*, attached to HPA 929616, WNRC.

57. Of the thirteen people who filed homestead claims in this area, only Arthur W. Brown failed to establish residence.

58. Statement of Mrs. LaRue Schulz, 3 June 1920, HPA 929616, WNRC; Transaction Records, SP. Presumably, Mrs. Schulz was either renting this quarter section from the Idaho man or had made arrangements (never finalized) to purchase the property from him.

59. *Nevada State Herald*, 2 July 1915; homesteaders' statements in various patent applications, particularly those of Fred Woods, 9 December 1915, HPA 517453; Edward J. Fitzgerald, 25 July 1916, HPA 551965; James P. Farley, 5 October 1917, HPA 623101; and Albert Bosley, 19 May 1920, HPA 770644, WNRC.

CHAPTER 3

1. Letters from Walter L. Fisher, Secretary of the Interior, to Tasker L. Oddie, Governor of Nevada, 26 October 1911 and 3 January 1912, with a map showing withdrawn land accompanying the second letter, MLC files, NHS; *Elko Free Press,* 24 November 1911.

2. Protest on Application for Permit to Appropriate the Public Waters of the State of Nevada, 8 April 1912, Folder 1807, Nevada Division of Water Resources (NDWR), Carson City; *Elko Free Press,* 2 June 1911, 19 April 1912, 26 April 1912, and 15 June 1915; *Nevada State Herald,* 19 April 1912, 26 April 1912, 3 May 1912, 24 May 1912, and 14 June 1912; Woelz, 6–7.

3. *Metropolis Chronicle,* 15 November 1912, 1 December 1912, 15 January 1913, and 1 April 1913; *Nevada State Herald,* 6 December 1912, 27 March 1913, and 13 June 1913. The hotel building would later be used by the people of Metropolis for various social functions, but it would never again be operated as a business establishment.

4. *Nevada State Herald,* 22 October 1915, 17 March 1916, 7 April 1916, 28 April 1916, and 7 September 1917; *Elko Free Press,* 1 February 1916 and 19 January 1917; letters from George C. Rice, President, Metropolis Land Co., to Nevada Bureau of Industry, Agriculture, and Irrigation, 17 April 1916; from the Bureau to Rice, 20 April 1916; and from C. L. Deady, State Land Register, to W. M. Wiley, Manager, Metropolis Land Co., 6 September 1917, MLC files, NHS. The broader implications of this activity are reviewed in Marshall E. Bowen, "A Backward Step: From Irrigation to Dry Farming in the Nevada Desert," *Agricultural History* 63 (Spring 1989): 231–242.

5. Homesteaders' statements in their HPAs, particularly that of John A. Bake, 3 April 1916, HPA 536414, WNRC; Elko County tax assessments, 1913 and 1915, ECCH; *Metropolis Chronicle,* 1 September 1912.

6. The emergence of dry farm landscapes in those parts of Cache Valley that lay beyond reach of irrigation water is described in Lamborn, 39–41; A. J. Simmonds, *On the Big Range: A Centennial History of Cornish and Trenton, Cache County, Utah, 1870–1890* (Logan: Utah State University Press, 1970), 53–55; and Larry D. Christiansen, "The History of Newton, Utah," (M.S. thesis, Utah State University, 1967), 38–39. These developments are placed within a broader regional context by Charles S. Peterson, who maintains that Cache Valley occupied a place within the "southern margins of . . . the northwestern wheat belt" and argues that the expansion of dry farming settlement, and the new rural landscapes that it created, brought the valley into closer conformity with other wheat-producing districts of the American West and set it apart from those parts of Utah still characterized by traditional Mormon villages. Peterson, "Imprint of Agricultural Systems," 102–103, and *Changing Times: A View from Cache Valley, 1890–1915* (Logan: Utah State University, 1979), 5.

7. Homesteaders' statements in their HPAs, WNRC; Elko County tax assessments, ECCH; Transaction Records, SP; *Nevada State Herald,* 23 July 1915.

8. Elko County tax assessments, 1915, ECCH.

9. *Nevada State Herald,* 11 July 1913, 21 November 1913, 27 February 1914, and 5 February 1915; *Elko Free Press,* 28 June 1916.

10. Homesteaders' statements in their HPAs, particularly those of John W. Luckart, 1 September 1916, HPA 558463, and 27 September 1918, HPA 703529; Charles N.

Luckart, 1 September 1916, HPA 558464; Benjamin F. Blaylock, Jr., 11 November 1916, HPA 577166; and Alma L. Montgomery, 21 October 1920, HPA 826498, WNRC. *Nevada State Herald,* 3 July 1914; *Elko Free Press,* 5 May 1915.

11. Elko County tax assessments, 1915, ECCH; statement of John W. Luckart, 21 July 1915, HPA 497437, WNRC.

12. Homesteaders' statements in their HPAs, WNRC; Storheim, "We Remember Metropolis, Nevada," and Eva Hyde Koyen, "Profiles of Wilford A. Hyde," in Holbrook, 22 and 27; Bertie Bake, "The History of My Home Town," General Collections, NHS; Blaylock Journal, 9–10 October 1913 and 1 July 1916, LDS; *Metropolis Chronicle,* 1 February 1913; *Nevada State Herald,* 18 April 1913 and 7 April 1916; *Elko Free Press,* 19 April 1916. Although most men obtained off-farm jobs in Utah and Nevada, some worked in Idaho and Wyoming, and a few ventured as far away as Alberta and Iowa.

13. Statements of Lytton Y. Mathews, 26 October 1914 and 4 August 1915, supplemented by statement of James H. Allen, 8 July 1915, and letter from Joseph Jensen, Mineral Inspector, GLO, to Commissioner, GLO, 23 September 1915, HPA 537753, WNRC; Mathews family genealogical records and Metropolis Ward Record of Members, LDS.

14. These events, which affected farms throughout northeastern Nevada, are discussed at length in Chapter Four.

15. Letters from George B. Standing, Cashier, Metropolis Land Co., to C. L. Deady, Carey Act Land Register, 20 September 1918; from William S. Hanson, General Manager, Metropolis Land Co., to Deady, 6 August 1920; and from Deady to Hanson, 11 August 1920, Pacific Reclamation Co. correspondence files, NHS. Letters from William Spry, Commissioner, GLO, to Nevada Commissioner of Industry, Agriculture and Irrigation, Dept. of Carey Act Lands, 19 January 1923, and from Deady to L. F. Hatch, Manager of the Metropolis Land Co., 3 February 1923, MLC files, NHS. H. M. Payne, Deputy State Engineer, memorandum of 16 February 1923, Folder 1807, NDWR.

16. *Elko Free Press,* 31 July 1917 and 7 November 1917; *Nevada State Herald,* 26 October 1917.

17. Metropolis Ward Manuscript History, LDS; *Elko Free Press,* 27 September 1920; *Nevada State Herald,* 18 March 1921 and 16 June 1922. By the turn of the century, dairying had begun to rival wheat production as Cache Valley's principal source of agricultural income. Lambert, who had spent many years in the valley before coming to Nevada, was familiar with both types of farming. Not only did he study dry farming at the Agricultural College, but for a time he also served as a dairy inspector in Cache County. Peterson, *Changing Times,* 13; *Logan Journal,* 28 September 1911.

18. *Nevada State Herald,* 14 April 1922, 21 April 1922, 16 June 1922, and 25 August 1922.

19. Statements by Hyde and Oscar S. Rice, 16 May 1919, HPA 713086; and letter from Palmer to Commissioner, GLO, 15 December 1922, attached to HPA 894007, WNRC.

20. Elko County tax assessments, 1922–1923, ECCH; letter from Palmer to Commissioner, GLO, 15 December 1922, attached to HPA 894007, WNRC.

21. J. Carlos Lambert, *The Metropolis Reclamation Project,* University of Nevada Agricultural Experiment Station Bulletin No. 107 (Reno: University of Nevada, November, 1924), 12–16. The number of Metropolis farmers in 1917 is derived from an accounting made by Lambert that was published in the *Nevada State Herald,* 7 September 1917. By 1923 only one farmer remained in Afton, still trying, without much success, to raise grain on a few dryland acres.

22. Lambert, 15–16; *Nevada State Herald*, 28 April 1922; *Elko Free Press*, 28 February 1923, 25 April 1923, and 14 November 1923. The one man who did not have an off-farm job in 1923 was able to earn a satisfactory living from the sale of cream, livestock (he owned thirty head of beef cattle in addition to his dairy cows), and wool, the latter accounting for nearly fifteen percent of his total cash sales.

23. Statements of Marion Barnes, 17 June 1916, HPA 550934, and Edward J. Fitzgerald, 25 July 1916, HPA 551965, WNRC.

24. Statements of Bertha Lenhart, 18 June 1914, HPA 438433; John C. Corbett, 18 June 1914, HPA 438434; and T. Wesley Tame, 29 October 1914, HPA 472547, WNRC.

25. Statement of William J. Quinn, 9 December 1915, HPA 517451, supplemented by those of Fred Woods, 9 December 1915, HPAs 517451 and 517453; Maude P. Peers, 9 December 1915, HPA 517451; Bertha Lenhart, 18 June 1914, HPA 438433; and John C. Corbett, 18 June 1914, HPA 438434, WNRC. *Climatic Summary,* data for Clover Valley and Wells; Elko County tax assessments, 1917–1918, ECCH; *Nevada State Herald,* 26 December 1913 and 10 July 1914; *Elko Free Press,* 24 February 1914. Fred Woods, who helped Quinn plow his land in 1912, was a native of Indiana who had lived in Elko County for several years, and was well acquainted with Nevada conditions. He was one of the few people who came to Tobar Flat adequately equipped with work stock and farming implements.

26. Homesteaders' statements in their HPAs, particularly that of T. Wesley Tame, 29 October 1914, HPA 472547, WNRC. This accounting does not include the slight success enjoyed by William J. Quinn, who, as noted earlier, had a "very light" crop in 1913, not a good result by any stretch of the imagination, but better than his absolute failures of 1911, 1912, and 1915.

27. Homesteaders' statements in their HPAs, particularly that of Joseph B. McDaniel, 28 July 1914, HPA 441336, WNRC; McDaniel interview, 4 July 1979.

28. Statements of Maude Byrne Sloan, 3 March 1920, HPA 777013, and John A. McRae, 3 June 1920, HPA 929616; letter from N. F. Waddell, Special Agent, GLO, to Commissioner, GLO, 9 March 1922, and testimony of Paul Striebel, Maude Byrne Sloan, John J. Sloan, John A. McRae, and Pete Bylund, 25 November 1922, in *U.S. v. McRae,* attached to HPA 929616, WNRC. Mrs. Byrne harvested garden vegetables in 1917 and 1919. It is impossible to determine the size of Koehler's grain field or the years in which he and Striebel got something to grow on their land because neither man "proved up," and thus left no systematic record of his yearly farming activities. Indirect evidence, supplied primarily by Striebel's testimony in *U.S. v. McRae,* suggests that Koehler cut hay from his grain field in either 1916 or 1919 and that Striebel's half-acre of wheat was grown in either 1916 or 1917.

29. Letter from James P. Farley to Clay Tallman, U.S. Land Commissioner, 11 August 1917, and statement of Farley, 5 October 1917, HPA 623101; letter from Watson J. Loveless to Tallman, 14 August 1917, and statement of Loveless, 5 October 1917, HPA 623102; and testimony of Paul Striebel, 25 November 1922, in *U.S. v. McRae,* attached to HPA 929616, WNRC.

30. Elko County tax assessments, 1911–1917, ECCH; testimony of Paul Striebel, 25 November 1922, in *U.S. v. McRae,* attached to HPA 929616, WNRC; McDaniel interview, 4 July 1979.

31. Testimony of John A. McRae and Paul Striebel, 25 November 1922, in *U.S. v. McRae*, attached to HPA 929616, WNRC.

32. *Nevada State Herald*, 7 April 1911, 25 August 1911, 3 October 1913, and 26 February 1915; McDaniel interview, 4 July 1979.

33. Homesteaders' statements in their HPAs, particularly those of T. Wesley Tame, 29 October 1914, HPA 472547; Edward J. Fitzgerald, 25 July 1916, HPA 551965; and Maude Byrne Sloan, 3 March 1920, HPA 777013; Waddell to Commissioner, 9 March 1922, in *U.S. v. McRae*, attached to HPA 929616, WNRC. Unpatented homestead files CC 05065, EL 01653, and EL 02025, BLM; *Nevada State Herald*, 25 August 1911; *Salt Lake City Directory*, 1913–1915.

34. Homesteaders' statements in their HPAs, particularly those of Marion Barnes, 17 June 1916, HPA 550934, and Edward J. Fitzgerald, 25 July 1916, HPA 551965; affidavit filed by Celsus P. Heidel, 26 January 1922; letter from E. N. Quinn, Special Agent, GLO, to J. H. Favorite, GLO, 28 January 1922; and testimony of Paul Striebel and John A. McRae in *U.S. v. McRae*, attached to HPA 929616, WNRC. Unpatented homestead files EL 01619, EL 01620, EL 01652, EL 01653, EL 01766, EL 01767, EL 01710, and EL 01729, BLM; McDaniel interview, 4 July 1979; Troxel interview, 20 July 1985.

35. *Nevada State Herald*, 11 September 1914, 24 November 1916, 30 March 1917, 25 May 1917, and 28 September 1917; *Elko Free Press*, 16 August 1916, 6 March 1917, 12 March 1917, 31 July 1917, 27 March 1918, 1 March 1922, 22 March 1922, 30 August 1922, and 6 May 1925. John Carlos Lambert, stationed at Metropolis, was instrumental in arranging many of these events, but it should be remembered that the initial steps were taken by the farmers themselves, almost three years before Lambert arrived in Nevada.

36. Metropolis Ward Manuscript History and the Metropolis Ward Historical Record (MWHR), 22 February 1912, 1 September 1912, 10 May 1914, and 24 September 1922, LDS; Holbrook, 8–9 and 28–32.

37. Blaylock Journal, 20 September 1914; Life Sketch of Benjamin Franklin Blaylock, Jr.; and MWHR, 11 May 1924, LDS.

38. MWHR, 13 April 1913, 15 August 1915, and 10 October, 1915, LDS; *Nevada State Herald*, 12 November 1915.

39. MWHR, 15 August 1915, LDS; *Elko Free Press*, 18 August 1917; *Nevada State Herald*, 23 November 1917, 18 October 1918, 30 January 1920, and 14 April 1922.

40. MWHR, 23 April 1930 and 5 May 1930, LDS; Metropolis Ward Manuscript History, 30 September 1934 and 31 December 1934, LDS; Holbrook, 14; Jensen interview, 27 June 1981.

41. MWHR, 3 November 1912, 2 March 1913, 17 May 1914, 18 July 1915, and 25 July 1915, LDS.

42. *Elko Free Press*, 23 May 1919 and 29 June 1921; *Nevada State Herald*, 24 March 1922 and 21 April 1922; Holbrook, 15.

43. MWHR, 7 March 1937, LDS.

44. *Elko Free Press*, 26 January 1916, 12 May 1916, 17 May 1922, 2 October 1922, 14 March 1923, 25 May 1923, and 4 January 1924; *Nevada State Herald*, 14 September 1923; Holbrook, 10–11; Jensen interview, 27 June 1981; author's interview with Mrs. Beth Roberts, a former member of the Metropolis High School girls' basketball team, Gridley, California, 27 June 1981.

45. *Metropolis Chronicle*, 25 November 1911, 15 January 1912, 1 April 1912, and 1 May 1912; *Nevada State Herald*, 5 January 1912, 9 February 1912, and 29 March 1912; *Elko Free Press*, 10 May 1912; *Metropolis Improvement Co.: Town Lots* (Salt Lake City: Metropolis Improvement Co., 1913); Nell Murbarger, *Ghosts of the Glory Trail* (Los Angeles: Westernlore Press, 1956; reprint ed., Las Vegas: Nevada Publications, 1983), 247; Holbrook, 7; Woelz, 6 and 9. The exact number of saloons at Metropolis in its earliest days is uncertain. Holbrook places the number at two, but Murbarger claims that there were five, and Woelz maintains that the number was seven, although he does not say if they were all in existence at the same time. A map of Metropolis, drawn in 1913 and reproduced in Sheerin, 109, identifies four small structures as "bars" and notes that another drinking establishment was located in the hotel but does not make it clear if they were all still in operation at this time.

46. *Nevada State Herald,* 29 June 1917, 30 January 1920, 5 November 1920, 9 September 1921, and 8 August 1922; *Elko Free Press,* 24 September 1920 and 3 May 1922; MWHR, 26 March 1922, 24 July 1922, and 24 September 1922, LDS; Holbrook, 9–11; Elko County tax assessments, 1913–1917, ECCH; Jensen interview, 27 June 1981.

47. See note 41, Chapter Two.

48. *Nevada State Herald*, 8 November 1912, 22 November 1912, 3 October 1913, and 24 March 1916. Campbell's lecture at Wells on 14 November 1912 was followed in succeeding days by speeches at Metropolis and Elko.

49. *Elko Free Press,* 24 February 1917.

50. MWHR, 1912–1930, and Metropolis Ward Record of Members, LDS; McElrath; McDaniel interview, 9 January 1980.

51. *Nevada State Herald*, 3 May 1912, 3 October 1913, and 28 October 1921; testimony of Mrs. Francis Merrill, 25 November 1922, and letter from John A. McRae to Assistant Commissioner, U.S. Land Office, 17 April 1922, in *U.S. v. McRae*, attached to HPA 929616, WNRC; Elko County tax assessments, 1916, ECCH; McDaniel interviews, 4 July 1979 and 9 January 1980; Troxel interview, 20 July 1985.

52. *Nevada State Herald*, 3 October 1913, 23 October 1914, and 1 January 1915; McElrath; William J. Tatomer, "Tobar: Forgotten Ghost Town," *Northeastern Nevada Historical Society Quarterly* 78:1 (Winter 1978): 4–6; letter from J. W. Kingsbury, Mineral Inspector, GLO, to Commissioner, GLO, 21 May 1913, attached to HPA 401131, WNRC; transaction records, SP. The Hoaglins did not get around to formally platting their townsite until 1918, when it was surveyed as "Clover City," a drastically scaled-down version of what they had originally laid out in 1913 and more in keeping with the actual extent of the town's built-up area. This action was not taken until the Hoaglins had made at least three unsuccessful attempts to sell their townsite to out-of-state investors. "Map of Clover City, Elko County, Nevada," surveyed by C. A. DeArmond at the request of A. B. Hoaglin, 30 October 1918, County Recorder's Office, ECCH; *Salt Lake Tribune,* 18 May 1913; *Elko Free Press,* 21 September 1915; *Nevada State Herald*, 4 January 1916.

53. Testimony recorded between January, 1915, and July, 1916, in Case File No. 2225, *Sweeney et al. v. Jasmin and Schrader*, District Court, Elko, Nevada, ECCH; *Nevada State Herald*, 23 October 1914 and 1 January 1915; *Elko Independent*, 23 October 1914, 17 March 1916, and 21 March 1916. It is unclear whether the men hired by Jaensch were moving the building onto the Hoaglins' townsite or taking it from the Hoaglins' prop-

erty to the Jaensch townsite. Court testimony indicates that the armed confrontation occurred on public land between the two competing townsites.

54. *Nevada State Herald*, 6 October 1922; McDaniel interview, 9 January 1980; Troxel interview, 20 July 1985.

55. Cornelius Hoaglin laid out the brothers' original townsite in 1913 and operated their office in Tobar, while George S. Hoaglin split his time between Nevada and a Salt Lake City real estate office. Until 1918, A. B. Hoaglin concentrated his activities in California, trying to interest people in purchasing farmland and townsite properties. *Nevada State Herald*, 3 October 1913 and 1 January 1915; statement of George S. Hoaglin, 8 February 1915, Contest No. 79, U.S. Land Office, Elko, Nevada, FARC; statement of E. E. Glaser, 17 November 1915, Case File No. 2472, *Tobar Lumber and Trading Co. v. Janett Lowell and Cornelius Hoaglin,* District Court, Elko, Nevada, ECCH; McElrath.

56. Populations of both towns were quite fluid, depending on prospects for economic growth in the area and the number of settlers on the land. Numbers even fluctuated with the seasons, as farm families moved into Metropolis in the winter and shysters planning to profit from the arrival of homeseekers descended upon Tobar in the spring. A rough estimate for 1915 through 1917, based on tax records, LDS files, voting lists, newspaper items, and interviews, would place the "permanent" population of the Metropolis townsite at somewhere around fifty and that of Tobar between seventy-five and a hundred.

57. *Nevada State Herald*, 1 January 1915, 26 February 1915, 23 April 1915, and 30 May 1915; *Elko Independent*, 4 February 1916 and 12 May 1916; *Reese River Reveille* (Austin, Nev.), 12 June 1915; unpatented homestead files EL 01667, EL 02160, and EL 02464, BLM; statement of Ludlow B. Glafcke, 6 January 1916, Contest No. 110, U.S. Land Office, Elko, Nevada, FARC; Elko County tax assessments, 1913–1919, ECCH; McElrath.

58. *Nevada State Herald*, 15 January 1915 and 26 February 1915; *Salt Lake City Directory,* 1903–1916; Pengelly interview, 16 July 1982; author's interview with Mr. Ed Glaser, son of Tobar's lumber dealer, Calhan, Colorado, 19 July 1985.

59. Tatomer, 7–8; McElrath; *Nevada State Herald*, 20 March 1914, 10 July 1914, 31 July 1914, 11 September 1914, 1 January 1915, 15 January 1915, 26 February 1915, 23 April 1915, 9 July 1915, 23 July 1915, 31 December 1915, 4 January 1916, 31 May 1918, and 23 August 1918; *Elko Free Press*, 21 September 1915 and 20 March 1918; Leonard W. Hoskins, "Almost Forgotten Money," *Northeastern Nevada Historical Society Quarterly* 2:4 (Spring 1972): 12; statements of E. E. Glaser, 17 November 1915, and Cornelius Hoaglin, 9 May 1916, and deposition filed by Janett W. Lowell, 7 September 1916, Case File No. 2472, *Tobar Lumber and Trading v. Lowell and Hoaglin,* ECCH.

60. *Nevada State Herald*, 1 January 1915 and 22 March 1918; *Elko Independent,* 19 March 1918 and 30 March 1918; statement of E. E. Glaser, 17 November 1915, Case File No. 2472, *Tobar Lumber and Trading v. Lowell and Hoaglin*, ECCH; statement of Ludlow B. Glafcke, 6 January 1916, Contest No. 110, U.S. Land Office, Elko, Nevada, FARC; Troxel interview, 20 July 1985.

61. Statements of Ludlow B. Glafcke, 7 April 1915, Contest No. 88, and 6 January 1916, Contest No. 110, and Wilbur C. Earhart, 4 February 1916, Contest No. 114, U.S. Land Office, Elko, Nevada, FARC; papers filed with the U.S. Land Office, 17 June 1916, HPA 550934, WNRC; *Nevada State Herald*, 1 January 1915, 30 April 1915, and 14 May 1915; *Elko Free Press,* 21 September 1915.

62. *Elko Independent,* 8 April 1919; *Nevada State Herald,* 25 April 1919; Elko County tax assessments, 1919, ECCH.

63. Charles Stewart Powell, "Depression Days in Tobar," *Northeastern Nevada Historical Society Quarterly* 78:4 (Fall 1978): 136–137; author's interview with Judge Joseph O. McDaniel, a Tobar Flat native and younger brother of William McDaniel, Elko, Nevada, 27 June 1979.

Chapter 4

1. The most complete source of information on these matters is the collection of papers in the Pacific Reclamation Company and Metropolis Land Company files, NHS.

2. *Climatic Summary,* data for Metropolis, Wells, and the State Agricultural Experiment Dry Farm; U.S. Department of Agriculture, Weather Bureau, *Climatological Data, Nevada Section,* July, 1915 (Reno: Weather Bureau Office, 1915), data for Clover Valley; Daily Meteorological Reports for the Elko station, on file at the National Weather Service Office in Elko (NWS); *Nevada State Herald,* 6 August 1915 and 3 September 1915.

3. Statements of Milton M. Whitenton, 15 September 1916, HPA 570009, and Walter H. L. Whitenton, 18 September 1916, HPA 558466, WNRC; *Nevada State Herald,* 2 July 1915, 6 August 1915, and 20 August 1915. The remark of the old rancher (Seneca Weeks) is contained in the July 2 issue.

4. *Climatic Summary,* data for Metropolis and Clover Valley; Daily Meteorological Reports for the Elko station, NWS.

5. Homesteaders' statements in their HPAs, particularly those of M. Mabel Root, 14 June 1918, HPA 668312, and Albert Bosley, 19 May 1920, HPA 770644, WNRC.

6. Statements of Felix P. Toone, 21 June 1917, HPA 605564, and Oscar Geertsen, 30 August 1919, HPA 787146; letter from Farley to Tallman, 11 August 1917, HPA 623101; and testimony of Paul Striebel, 25 November 1922, in *U.S. v. McRae,* attached to HPA 929616, WNRC. *Elko Free Press,* 8 August 1916. The Clover Valley weather station recorded freezing temperatures on 22 June 1916 and again on 10 September, while Elko experienced below-zero weather on three successive days in early November. *Climatic Summary,* data for Clover Valley, and Daily Meteorological Reports, NWS.

7. R. A. Ward, *Control of the Jack-Rabbit Pest in Nevada,* Agricultural Extension Service Bulletin No. 13 (Reno: University of Nevada, 1917), 4; author's interview with Mr. Cliff Hepworth, Metropolis, Nevada, 24 August 1976. Luckart's observations were reported in the *Nevada State Herald,* 22 July 1915, while Mrs. Byrne's crop report is recorded in her statement of 3 March 1920, HPA 777013, WNRC.

8. This campaign developed in response to the threat posed by bands of rabid coyotes, which had been attacking cattle, sheep, and humans in northern Nevada and adjacent states. Federal and state agencies sent hunters and men equipped with poison into the rangelands to destroy the coyotes, with some of the greatest activity occurring northwest of Afton. From January to June, 1916, these men killed approximately thirty-three thousand coyotes. The campaign is summarized in Marshall Bowen, "Jackrabbit Invasion of a Nevada Agricultural Community," *Ecumene* 12 (October 1980): 8–9.

9. Ward, 4; *Elko Free Press,* 17 August 1917; Bowen, "Jackrabbit Invasion," 8–10.

10. Homesteaders' statements in their HPAs, WNRC; *Elko Free Press,* 20 June 1917 and 7 November 1917.

11. Statements of Adna Ferrin, 11 April 1918, HPA 668302; Frederick Calton, 8 August 1919, HPA 840195; and Oscar Geertsen, 30 August 1919, HPA 787146, WNRC. *Elko Free Press*, 23 May 1919. There is less evidence that farmers on Tobar Flat refrained from planting crops because of the probability of damage from rabbits and/or squirrels. One man who did follow this procedure was Burt Bosley, the butcher from Salt Lake City, who saw his 1915 and 1916 grain crops eaten by rabbits before losing his 1917 crop to an unspecified adversary. Bosley did not plant anything in 1918, but the next year, when rabbits seemed to be less numerous, he resumed farming and put forty acres in crops. Statement of Albert Bosley, 19 May 1920, HPA 770644, WNRC, supplemented by an item in the *Nevada State Herald*, 20 June 1919.

12. Homesteaders' statements in their HPAs, particularly those of Donna B. Green, 12 April 1919, HPA 704576, and Winslow L. Farr, 20 December 1919, HPA 753028, and Charles B. Farr, 20 November 1919, HPA 752609; and testimony of Paul Striebel, 25 November 1922, in *U.S. v. McRae*, attached to HPA 929616, WNRC.

13. Ball et al, in *The 1921 Yearbook of Agriculture*, 138–141; O. E. Baker, "A Graphic Summary of American Agriculture," in *The 1921 Yearbook of Agriculture*, 528; Jensen interview, 27 June 1981; William McDaniel interview, 4 July 1979.

14. Homesteaders' statements in their HPAs, particularly those of Philip G. Hill and William T. Hill, 22 April 1916, HPA 536415; John W. Luckart, 27 September 1918, HPA 703529; and Watson J. Loveless in his letter of 14 August 1917 to Clay Tallman, U.S. Land Commissioner, HPA 623102, WNRC. *Nevada State Herald*, 31 December 1915, 4 February 1916, 11 February 1916, 23 September 1921, and 4 April 1924; *Elko Free Press*, 11 August 1920; *John Anthony Woolf Family Life Histories,* 235–236; Storheim, "We Remember," in Holbrook, 24.

15. Homesteaders' statements in their HPAs, particularly those of Horton H. Hammond, 28 September 1915, HPA 504973; Alma Balls, 28 September 1915, HPA 504974; James O. Nielson, 10 November 1915, HPA 510256; and Oscar L. Rice, 10 November 1915, HPA 510259, WNRC. *Nevada State Herald,* 20 August 1915. The estimate of wheat yields needed by dry farmers to break even is found in the *Nevada State Herald,* 10 September 1915.

16. Statements of James H. Allen, 23 July 1915, and William H. Hepworth, 12 September 1915, in MWHR, LDS; *Nevada State Herald,* 20 August 1915 and 16 March 1917.

17. Homesteaders' statements in their HPAs, WNRC; *Nevada State Herald,* 27 April 1917 and 31 July 1917; *Elko Free Press,* 7 November 1917; Jensen interview, 27 June 1981.

18. Homesteaders' statements in their HPAs, particularly those of William Barrows, 23 April 1919, HPA 703528, and Annie M. Hyde, 31 March 1921, HPA 830874, WNRC; *Nevada State Herald,* 5 July 1918.

19. Bishop Simpson M. Woolf, quoted in the *Elko Free Press,* 23 May 1919; *Nevada State Herald*, 20 June 1919.

20. Settlers' statements in their HPAs, WNRC. The only person who practiced summer fallowing on Tobar Flat in 1915 was Henry E. Boehme, who had taken over a homestead abandoned by one of the Salt Lake City people in 1914. Boehme planted wheat and barley on this land in 1916, but by July he could see that the grain was "burning and will

not make a crop," a clear sign that summer fallowing had not worked. Statement of Henry E. Boehme, 25 July 1916, HPA 555012, WNRC.

21. Statements of Joseph H. Parkin and John J. Kinney, 14 December 1915, HPA 517455, WNRC; *Elko Free Press,* 22 October 1915 and 3 November 1915; *Elko Independent,* 4 February 1916 and special Industrial Issue, August 1916; McElrath.

22. *Nevada State Herald,* 24 March 1916; *Elko Independent,* special Industrial Issue, August 1916; McElrath. All but one of the fourteen homesteaders who specified depths of domestic wells in their HPAs indicated that they had to dig between six and twenty feet to reach water, with the median depth of water recorded at fourteen feet. In contrast, the four irrigation wells whose depths are known reached water between eighty and one hundred feet below the surface.

23. Statements of Joseph H. Parkin, 14 December 1915, HPA 517455; Edward Wardvogel, 14 June 1916, HPA 551968; Alma K. Stroud, 12 July 1918, HPA 668317; James Bissell, 7 April 1919, HPA 703534; and Albert Bosley, 19 May 1920, HPA 770644, WNRC. Unpatented homestead files EL 01488, EL 01610, EL 01710, EL 02917, and EL 02971, BLM; Elko County tax assessments, 1916–1917, ECCH; William McDaniel interview, 9 January 1980.

24. Statement of James Bissell, 7 April 1919, HPA 703534, WNRC; Pengelly interview, 22 June 1982; Elko County tax assessments, 1917–1920, ECCH.

25. MWHR, 15 August 1915 and 10 October 1915, LDS; *Nevada State Herald,* 10 December 1915, 17 December 1915, and 26 January 1917.

26. The Metropolis rabbit drives of 1917–1918 are described in Bowen, "Jackrabbit Invasion," 10–13, which draws heavily from items in the *Nevada State Herald* and the *Elko Free Press.*

27. Homesteaders' statements in their HPAs, particularly those of John A. Tate, 26 June 1916, HPA 550945; Edward J. Fitzgerald, 25 July 1916, HPA 551965; James Bissell, 7 April 1919, HPA 703534; Donna B. Green, 12 April 1919, HPA 704576; Herman H. Schrader, 30 June 1919, HPA 715492; and Jessie E. Ware, 3 July 1919, HPA 718166, WNRC. William McDaniel interviews, 4 July 1979 and 9 January 1980.

28. Homesteaders' statements in their HPAs, particularly that of William F. Schroeder, 19 July 1918, HPA 668319; affidavit filed by Celsus P. Heidel, 26 January 1922, in *U.S. v. McRae,* attached to HPA 929616, WNRC.

29. Statement of Maude Byrne Sloan, 3 March 1920, HPA 777013, supplemented by testimony of Paul Striebel, 25 November 1922, in *U.S. v. McRae,* attached to HPA 929616, WNRC; William McDaniel interview, 4 July 1979.

30. Statements of Clarence M. Barton and Joseph B. McDaniel, 17 September 1915, HPA 510255; William J. Blackwell, 8 October 1918, HPA 703534; Donna B. Green, 12 April 1919, HPA 704573; and Amos C. West, 4 April 1921, HPA 819596, WNRC.

31. The invasion of ground squirrels at Metropolis brought about a new round of farmers' meetings and poisoning campaigns organized by the church, which is documented by the *Nevada State Herald* and the *Elko Free Press,* 1919–1920. By late 1921 the number of squirrels had been greatly reduced, prompting a man living near Metropolis to write that "after the expiration of two years, the pests have been exterminated to a great extent, [which] will justify me in attempting to raise a crop." Statement of Rueben A. Jensen, 19 December 1921, HPA 854185, WNRC.

32. U.S. Census of Population, supplemented by GLO and LDS materials and Elko County tax assessments, ECCH.

33. Principal sources include various Mormon church records, GLO files, Elko County tax assessments, newspaper items, and old timers' recollections.

34. Metropolis Ward Record of Members; Blaylock, Montgomery, Storey, and Whitenton family genealogical records, LDS; Life Sketch of Benjamin Franklin Blaylock, Jr., LDS; Elko County tax assessments, 1920–1925, ECCH.

35. Andrew Jenson, "Flourishing Branch in Northern California," *Deseret Evening News,* 23 October 1915; Morgan, 336; Metropolis Ward Record of Members, MWHR, 20 April 1930 and 27 July 1930, and family genealogical records, LDS; Jensen interview, 27 June 1981. Even today, an annual "Metropolis families" picnic is held at Gridley, attended by a few surviving old timers from Nevada and a large number of their descendants.

36. *Nevada State Herald,* 28 February 1923 and 3 April 1925; *Elko Free Press,* 6 May 1925; Metropolis Ward Record of Members and family genealogical records, LDS; Pengelly interview, 22 June 1982; and Jensen interview, 27 June 1981.

37. Elko County tax assessments, 1915–1925, ECCH; *Salt Lake City Directory,* 1915–1916; *Denver Directory* (Denver: Will H. Richards, 1916–1925); Metropolis Ward Record of Members, LDS; *The Wickizer Annals,* 7.

38. Elko County tax assessments, 1915–1925, ECCH; letter from John A. McRae to Assistant Commissioner, U.S. Land Office, 17 April 1922, and statement of John A. McRae, 25 November 1922, in *U.S. v. McRae,* attached to HPA 929616, WNRC.

39. Statements by M. Mabel Root, Herman H. Schrader, and James Bissell, 14 June 1918, HPA 668312, WNRC; *Utah State Gazetteer and Business Directory,* 1912–1913; Elko County tax assessments, 1920–1928, ECCH.

40. Elko County tax assessments, 1925–1928, ECCH.

41. The 1920s movement to California, and to the Los Angeles area in particular, is described in Kevin Starr, *Material Dreams: Southern California Through the 1920s* (New York: Oxford University Press, 1990), 65–89, and Robert M. Fogelson, *The Fragmented Metropolis: Los Angeles, 1850–1930* (Cambridge: Harvard University Press, 1967), 74–84. Danbom, 134–136, places the flight from farms to cities within a national context, and observes that the new arrivals from rural America were now competing with immigrants for unskilled jobs in the rapidly growing cities.

42. GLO tract books and homesteaders' statements in their HPAs, particularly those of Alma K. Stroud, 7 June 1918, HPA 668317; M. Mabel Root and Herman H. Schrader, 14 June 1918, HPA 668312; and George S. Hoaglin, 19 July 1918, HPA 668319, WNRC. *Nevada State Herald,* 3 October 1913 and 1 January 1915; *Elko Independent,* 14 June 1918; *Milo* (Iowa) *Motor,* 12 November 1908 and 26 January 1911; *Los Angeles City Directory,* 1912–1914; Transaction Records, SP. Herman H. Schrader and Will Schroeder grew up near Milo, Iowa, whose weekly paper, the *Motor,* regularly printed items about former residents of the area who had moved to California and other distant places.

43. Elko County tax assessments, 1916–1924, ECCH; statement of Clarence Barton, 12 May 1920, HPA 770644; and affidavit filed by Celsus P. Heidel, 26 January 1922, and letter from E. N. Quinn, Special Agent, GLO, to J. H. Favorite, GLO, both in *U.S. v. McRae,* attached to HPA 929616, WNRC. Tame, Parkin, and Moss family genealogical records, LDS; *Deseret Evening News,* 18 August 1953; *Salt Lake City Directory,* 1915–1925; *Denver Directory,* 1916–1930; author's interviews with Mr. Leo Wickizer, son of one Tobar Flat

settler and nephew of another, Stratton, Nebraska, 22 August 1985, and with Mrs. Jean Kerr, granddaughter of a Tobar Flat settler, Woods Cross, Utah, 19 July 1982.
44. Holbrook, 11–14; Morgan, 330–336; Metropolis Ward Historical Statistics, Record of Members, and Historical Record, 1930–1949, LDS.
45. MWHR, 24 April 1949, LDS.

CHAPTER 5

1. Twentieth-century pioneering on the plateaus of Utah and New Mexico is discussed in Charles S. Peterson, *Look to the Mountains: Southeastern Utah and the LaSal National Forest* (Provo: Brigham Young University Press, 1975), 157–165; Melvin J. Frost, "Factors that Influenced Homesteading and Land Abandonment in San Juan County, Utah" (M.S. thesis, Brigham Young University, 1960); and Evon Z. Vogt, *Modern Homesteaders: The Life of a Twentieth-Century Frontier Community* (Cambridge: Harvard University Press, 1955). Conditions around the Big Bend are described in George Macinko, "The Ebb and Flow of Wheat Farming in the Big Bend, Washington," *Agricultural History* 59 (April 1985): 215–228. For the West River country, see Nelson, *After the West Was Won*, supplemented by Jeffrey B. Roet, "Agricultural Settlement on the Dry Farming Frontier, 1900–1920" (Ph.D. dissertation, Northwestern University, 1982), 169–179. Each of these studies provides a good picture of pioneer life, but only Roet touches upon the existence of significant spatial contrasts.
2. This view differs slightly from that set forth by Paul Voisey in his study of the early twentieth-century farmers' frontier in southern Alberta. Voisey argues that no single theory or model can adequately explain the complexities of homestead and community life, especially when these are examined at the local level. Instead, he suggests that physical environment, frontier conditions, metropolitan influences, and cultural heritage combined to produce distinctive patterns of life and landscape as pioneer society took shape. Paul Voisey, *Vulcan: The Making of a Prairie Community* (Toronto: University of Toronto Press, 1988), 247–254.
3. Evon Z. Vogt and Thomas F. O'Dea, "A Comparative Study of the Role of Values in Social Action in Two Southwestern Communities," *American Sociological Review* 18 (December 1953): 645–654.
4. Vogt and O'Dea, 650–651. This same theme is brought out by Vogt within a broader cultural context in "Ecology and Economy," Chapter Six in Evon Z. Vogt and Ethel M. Albert, eds., *People of Rimrock: A Study of Values in Five Cultures* (Cambridge: Harvard University Press, 1966), 160–190.

Bibliography

Primary Sources

MANUSCRIPTS AND MANUSCRIPT COLLECTIONS

Bake, Bertie. "The History of My Home Town." Nevada Historical Society, Reno.

Blaylock, Benjamin F. Daily Journal, 1881–1929. Church of Jesus Christ of Latter-day Saints, Historical Department, Salt Lake City, Utah.

Blaylock, Jr., Benjamin Franklin. Life Sketch. Church of Jesus Christ of Latter-day Saints, Historical Department, Salt Lake City, Utah.

Church of Jesus Christ of Latter-day Saints, Genealogical Library, Salt Lake City, Utah. Family Genealogical Records.

Church of Jesus Christ of Latter-day Saints, Historical Department, Salt Lake City, Utah. Metropolis Ward Historical Record, 1912–1949.

Church of Jesus Christ of Latter-day Saints, Historical Department, Salt Lake City, Utah. Metropolis Ward Historical Statistics.

Church of Jesus Christ of Latter-day Saints, Historical Department, Salt Lake City, Utah. Metropolis Ward Record of Members, 1912–1935.

Church of Jesus Christ of Latter-day Saints, Historical Department, Salt Lake City, Utah. North Ogden Ward Historical Record, 1910–1912.

Elko, Nevada. Elko County Court House. Elko County Tax Assessments, 1908–1930.

Elko, Nevada. Elko County Court House. Elko District Court Case Files.

Elko, Nevada. Elko County Court House. "Map of Clover City, Nevada" (1918).

Elko, Nevada. Elko County Court House. "Map of Metropolis, Nevada" (1911).

Elko, Nevada. Elko County Court House. "[Map of] Tobar Townsite, Elko County, Nevada" (1911).

Federal Archives and Record Center, San Bruno, California. Minutes of Proceedings, Contest Dockets, Carson City and Elko Land Offices. Record Group 49.

Metropolis Land Company Files. Nevada Historical Society, Reno.

National Archives, Washington, D.C. U.S. Census of Population, Manuscript Schedules for 1900 and 1910.

National Weather Service, Elko, Nevada. Daily Meteorological Reports, 1888–1950.

Nevada Division of Water Resources, Carson City, Nevada. Applications to Appropriate the Public Waters of the State of Nevada.

Pacific Reclamation Company Files. Nevada Historical Society, Reno, Nevada.

"Some of John and Laura Churchfield's History." Papers in possession of Mr. and Mrs. Sim Churchfield, Elko, Nevada.

Southern Pacific Land Company, San Francisco. Transaction Records.

U.S. Bureau of Land Management, Reno, Nevada. Unpatented Homestead Files, Carson City and Elko Land Offices.

Utah. Office of the Secretary of State, Salt Lake City. Articles of Incorporation of Tobar Mercantile Company.

Washington National Records Center, Suitland, Maryland. General Land Office Serial Patent Files (Homestead Patent Applications). Record Group 49.

Washington National Records Center, Suitland, Maryland. General Land Office Tract Books. Record Group 49.

Western Pacific Files. California Historical Society, San Francisco.

CONTEMPORARY GOVERNMENT PUBLICATIONS

Farrell, F.D. *Dry-land Grains in the Great Basin.* U.S. Department of Agriculture, Bureau of Plant Industry Circular No. 61. Washington: Government Printing Office, 1910.

Lambert, J. Carlos. *The Metropolis Reclamation Project.* University of Nevada Agricultural Experiment Station Bulletin No. 107. Reno: University of Nevada, November, 1924.

Scofield, Carl S. *Dry Farming in the Great Basin.* U.S. Department of Agriculture, Bureau of Plant Industry Bulletin No. 103. Washington: Government Printing Office, 1907.

U.S. Department of Agriculture. *Climatological Data, Nevada Section, July, 1915.* Reno: Weather Bureau Office, 1915.

———. *The 1921 Yearbook of Agriculture.* Washington: Government Printing Office, 1922.

Ward, R.A. *Control of the Jack-Rabbit Pest in Nevada.* Agricultural Extension Service Bulletin No. 13. Reno: University of Nevada, 1917.

Widstoe, John A., and Lewis A. Merrill. *Arid Farming in Utah: First Report of the State Experimental Arid Farms.* Experiment Station Bulletin No. 91. Logan: The Agricultural College of Utah, 1905.

Zapoleon, L.B. *Geography of Wheat Prices.* U.S. Department of Agriculture Bulletin No. 594. Washington: Government Printing Office, 1918.

NEWSPAPERS

Box Elder News (Brigham City, Utah), 1907–1919.
Deseret Church News, 2 September 1989.
Deseret Evening News, 23 October 1915, 1 November 1932, 18 August 1953, and 17 February 1970.
Elko Free Press, 1911–1926 and 4 May 1949.
Elko Independent, 1914–1919.
Idaho Enterprise (Malad), 1909–1915.
Logan Journal, 1909–1911.
Metropolis Chronicle, 1911–1913.
Milo Motor (Milo, Iowa), 1908–1912.
Nevada State Herald (Wells), 1903–1926.
Nevada State Journal (Reno), 21 May 1961.
Ogden Standard, 1910–1911.
Reese River Reveille (Austin, Nevada), 12 June 1915.
Salt Lake Tribune, 1911–1917 and 4 October 1953.

INTERVIEWS BY AUTHOR

Churchfield, Sim, son of a Tobar Flat settler. Elko, Nevada, 26 June 1979 and 16 July 1982.
Glaser, Ed, son of a Tobar lumber dealer. Calhan, Colorado, 19 July 1985.
Hepworth, Cliff, lifelong resident of Metropolis. Metropolis, Nevada, 24 August 1976.
Jensen, Clifford, former Mormon bishop of Metropolis. Gridley, California, 27 June 1981.
Kerr, Jean, granddaughter of a Tobar Flat settler. Woods Cross, Utah, 19 July 1982.
McDaniel, Joseph O., son of a Tobar Flat settler. Elko, Nevada, 27 June 1979.
McDaniel, William, son of a Tobar Flat settler. McGill, Nevada, 4 July 1979 and 9 January 1980.
McQueen, Nettie, daughter of a Tobar Flat settler. Salt Lake City, Utah, 19 July 1982.
Pengelly, Eugene, former mayor of Wells and personal friend of many settler families. Wells, Nevada, 23 July 1981, 22 June 1982, 14 July 1982, 16 July 1982, and 17 July 1982.
Roberts, Beth, former resident of Metropolis. Gridley, California, 27 June 1981.
Troxel, Opal, daughter of a Tobar Flat settler. Wauneta, Nebraska, 20 July 1985.
Wickizer, Leo, son of a Tobar Flat settler. Stratton, Nebraska, 22 August 1985.

OTHER PRIMARY SOURCES

Denver City Directory. Denver: Ballenger and Richards, 1911–1930.
Farm Lands: Metropolis, Nevada. Salt Lake City: Pacific Reclamation Co., 1911.
Insurance Maps of Salt Lake City, Utah. New York: Sanborn Map Co., 1911.
Logan City and Cache County Directory. Salt Lake City: R.L. Polk and Co., 1909–1914.
Los Angeles City Directory. Los Angeles City Directory Co., 1911–1914.
Metropolis Improvement Co.: Town Lots. Salt Lake City: Metropolis Improvement Co., 1913.
Ogden City Directory. Salt Lake City: R.L. Polk and Co., 1908–1918.
Salt Lake City Directory. Salt Lake City: R.L. Polk and Co., 1900–1925.
San Francisco City Directory. San Francisco: H.S. Crocker Co., 1912.
The Colorado State Business Directory. Denver: The Gazetteer Publishing Co., 1913–1924.
Utah State Gazetteer and Business Directory. Salt Lake City: R.L. Polk and Co., 1900–1919.

SECONDARY SOURCES

Alexander, Thomas G., and James B. Allen. *Mormons and Gentiles: A History of Salt Lake City.* Boulder: Pruett Publishing Co., 1984.
Allen, Barbara. *Homesteading The High Desert.* Salt Lake City: University of Utah Press, 1987.
Arrington, Leonard J. *Great Basin Kingdom: An Economic History of the Latter-day Saints, 1830–1900.* Cambridge: Harvard University Press, 1958.
Badt, Gertrude N. "Milton Benjamin Badt." *Northeastern Nevada Historical Society Quarterly* 78:3 (Summer 1978): 90–112.
Bieder, Robert E. "Kinship as a Factor in Migration." *Journal of Marriage and the Family* 35 (August 1973): 429–439.
Bogue, Allan G. *From Prairie to Corn Belt: Farming on the Illinois and Iowa Prairies in the Nineteenth Century.* Chicago: University of Chicago Press, 1963.
———. *Money at Interest: The Farm Mortgage on the Middle Border.* Ithaca: Cornell University Press, 1955.
Bowen, Marshall E. "A Backward Step: From Irrigation to Dry Farming in the Nevada Desert." *Agricultural History* 63 (Spring 1989): 231–242.
———. "Elko County's Dry Farming Experimental Station." *Northeastern Nevada Historical Society Quarterly* 79:2 (Spring 1979): 34–51.
———. "Jackrabbit Invasion of a Nevada Agricultural Community." *Ecumene* 12 (October 1980): 6–16.

——. "Promoters and Pioneers: A Perspective on the Settlement Process in the Utah-Nevada Borderlands." *Pioneer America Society Transactions* 15 (1992): 23–31.

——. "The Desert Homestead as a Non-Farm Residence." *Nevada Historical Society Quarterly* 31 (Fall 1988): 198–211.

Bowers, William L. *The Country Life Movement in America, 1900–1920.* Port Washington, N.Y.: Kennikat Press, 1974.

Bowman, Isaiah. *The Pioneer Fringe.* American Geographical Society Special Publication No. 13. New York: American Geographical Society, 1931.

Brimlow, George F. *Harney County, Oregon, and Its Rangeland.* Portland: Binfords and Mort, 1951; reprint ed., Burns, Oreg.: Harney County Historical Society, 1980.

Buckles, James Slama. "The Historical Geography of the Fort Rock Valley, 1900–1941." M.A. thesis, University of Oregon, 1959.

Burgess, Mary Wickizer. *The Wickizer Annals.* San Bernardino, Calif: The Borgo Press, 1983.

Climatological Summary, Wells, Nevada. Reno: University of Nevada, College of Agriculture, 1970.

Christiansen, Larry D. "The History of Newton, Utah." M.S. thesis, Utah State University, 1967.

Culmsee, Carlton. "Last Free Land Rush." *Utah Historical Quarterly* 49 (Winter 1981): 26–41.

Danbom, David B. *The Resisted Revolution: Urban America and the Industrialization of Agriculture, 1900–1930.* Ames: Iowa State University Press, 1979.

De Nevi, Don. *The Western Pacific.* Seattle: Superior Publishing Co., 1978.

Eggleston, Dale C. "Harney County, Oregon : Some Aspects of Sequent Occupancy and Land Use." M.A. thesis, University of Oregon, 1970.

Fogelson, Robert M. *The Fragmented Metropolis: Los Angeles, 1850–1930.* Cambridge: Harvard University Press, 1967.

Frost, Melvin J. "Factors that Influenced Homesteading and Land Abandonment in San Juan County, Utah." M.S. thesis, Brigham Young University, 1960.

Gates, Paul W. *History of Public Land Law Development.* Washington: U.S. Government Printing Office, 1968.

Goldberg, Robert Alan. *Back to the Soil: The Jewish Farmers of Clarion, Utah, and Their World.* Salt Lake City: University of Utah Press, 1986.

Hargreaves, Mary Wilma M. *Dry Farming in the Northern Great Plains, 1900–1925.* Cambridge: Harvard University Press, 1957.

Hatton, Raymond R. *High Desert of Central Oregon.* Portland: Binfords and Mort, 1977.

Holbrook, Marjorie H. *History of Metropolis, Nevada.* Privately printed, 1986.

Hoskins, Leonard W. "Almost Forgotten Money." *Northeastern Nevada Historical Society Quarterly* 2:4 (Spring 1972): 5–13.

Houghton, John G., Clarence M. Sakamoto, and Richard O. Gifford. *Nevada's Weather and Climate*. Nevada Bureau of Mines and Geology Special Publication 2. Reno: University of Nevada, Mackay School of Mines, 1975.

Jackman, E.R., and R.A. Long. *The Oregon Desert*. Caldwell, Idaho: Caxton Printers 1967.

Jackson, Richard H., ed. *The Mormon Role in the Settlement of the West*. Provo: Brigham Young University Press, 1978.

Jensen, William R. "Canals and Canards: Three Case Studies of Land and Water Speculation in Utah, 1905–1920." M.S. thesis, Utah State University, 1971.

John Anthony Woolf Family Life Histories. Salt Lake City: John Anthony Woolf Family Organization, 1986.

Lamborn, John Edwin. "A History of the Development of Dry-Farming in Utah and Southern Idaho." M.A. thesis, Utah State University, 1978.

Layton, Stanford J. *To No Privileged Class: The Rationalization of Homesteading and Rural Life in the Early Twentieth-Century American West*. Provo: Brigham Young University, Charles Redd Center for Western Studies, 1988.

Lund, John Farnsworth. "The Night Before Doomsday." *Utah Historical Quarterly* 51 (Spring 1983): 154–161.

Macinko, George. "The Ebb and Flow of Wheat Farming in the Big Bend, Washington." *Agricultural History* 59 (April 1985): 215–228.

McCormick, John S. *The Historic Buildings of Downtown Salt Lake City*. Salt Lake City: Utah State Historical Society, 1982.

———. "Red Lights in Zion: Salt Lake City's Stockade, 1908–11." Utah Historical Quarterly 50 (Spring 1982): 168–181.

McElrath, Jean. "The Sign Pointed Thirsty 'to Bar.'" *Nevada State Journal*, 21 May 1961.

Meinig, D.W. "The Mormon Culture Region: Strategies and Patterns in the Geography of the American West, 1847–1964." *Annals of the Association of American Geographers* 55 (June 1965): 191–220.

Mifflin, M.D., and M.M. Wheat. *Pluvial Lakes and Estimated Pluvial Climates of Nevada*. Nevada Bureau of Mines and Geology Bulletin 94. Reno: University of Nevada, Mackay School of Mines, 1979.

Moran, William L. "A Dam in the Desert: Pat Moran's Last Water Venture." *Utah Historical Quarterly* 50 (Winter 1982): 22–39.

Morgan, Dale L. *The Humboldt: Highroad of the West*. New York: Farrar and Rinehart, 1943.

Murbarger, Nell. *Ghosts of the Glory Trail*. Los Angeles: Westernlore Press, 1956; reprint ed., Las Vegas: Nevada Publications, 1983.

Myrick, David F. *Railroads of Nevada and Eastern California*. Vol. 1, *The Northern Roads*. Berkeley: Howell-North Books, 1962.

———. *Railroads of Nevada and Eastern California*. Vol. 2, *The Southern Roads*. Berkeley: Howell-North Books, 1963.

Nelson, Paula M. *After the West Was Won: Homesteaders and Town-Builders in Western South Dakota, 1900–1917*. Iowa City: University of Iowa Press, 1986.

Noel, Thomas J. *The City and the Saloon: Denver, 1858–1916*. Lincoln: University of Nebraska Press, 1982.

Northeastern Nevada Cooperative Land-Use Study. Washington: U.S. Department of Agriculture, Soil Conservation Service, 1939.

Patterson, Edna B., Louise A. Ulph, and Victor Goodwin. *Nevada's Northeast Frontier*. Sparks, NV: Western Printing and Publishing Co., 1969.

Peffer, E. Louise. *The Closing of the Public Domain: Disposal and Reservation Polices, 1900–1950*. Stanford: Stanford University Press, 1951; reprint ed., New York: Arno Press, 1972.

Peterson, Charles S. *Changing Times: A View from Cache Valley, 1890–1915*. Logan: Utah State University, 1979.

———. *Look to the Mountains: Southeastern Utah and the LaSal National Forest*. Provo: Brigham Young University Press, 1975.

Powell, Charles Stewart. "Depression Days in Tobar." *Northeastern Nevada Historical Society Quarterly* 78:4 (Fall 1978): 127–140.

Proceedings of the Trans-Missouri Dry Farming Congress. Denver: Denver Chamber of Commerce, 1907.

Roet, Jeffrey B. "Agricultural Settlement on the Dry Farming Frontier, 1900–1920." Ph.D. dissertation, Northwestern University, 1982.

Scott, Roy V. *Railroad Development Programs in the Twentieth Century*. Ames: Iowa State University Press, 1985.

Sheerin, Chris H. "Three Who Dared: J. Selby Badt, 'Van,' and Ula Vandiver." *Northeastern Nevada Historical Society Quarterly* 80:4 (Fall 1980): 98–113.

Sherlock, Richard. "Mormon Migration and Settlement after 1875." *Journal of Mormon History* 2 (1975): 53–68.

Shideler, James H. *Farm Crisis, 1919–1923*. Berkeley: University of California Press, 1957.

Simmonds, A. J. *On the Big Range: A Centennial History of Cornish and Trenton, Cache County, Utah, 1870–1970*. Logan: Utah State University Press, 1970.

Snyder, C. T., George Hardman, and F. F. Zdenek. *Pleistocene Lakes in the Great Basin*. Miscellaneous Geologic Investigations, Map I-416. Washington: U.S. Geological Survey, 1964.

Starr, Kevin. *Material Dreams: Southern California Through the 1920s*. New York: Oxford University Press, 1990.

Stipanovich, Joseph. *The South Slavs in Utah: A Social History*. San Francisco: R and E Research Associates, 1975.

Tatomer, William J. "Tobar: Forgotten Ghost Town." *Northeastern Nevada Historical Society Quarterly* 78:1 (Winter 1978): 3–12.

Townley, John M. *Alfalfa Country: Nevada Land, Water, and Politics in the Nineteenth Century.* Reno: University of Nevada, Max C. Fleischmann College of Agriculture, 1981.

———. *Turn this Water into Gold: The Story of the Newlands Project.* Reno: Nevada Historical Society, 1977.

U.S. Department of Agriculture. *Climatic Summary of the United States.* Washington: U.S. Government Printing Office, 1932.

Vogt, Evon Z. *Modern Homesteaders: The Life of a Twentieth-Century Frontier Community.* Cambridge: Harvard University Press, 1955.

———, and Ethel M. Albert, eds. *People of Rimrock: A Study of Values in Five Cultures.* Cambridge: Harvard University Press, 1966.

———, and Thomas F. O'Dea. "A Comparative Study of the Role of Values in Social Action in Two Southwestern Communities." *American Sociological Review* 18 (December 1953): 645–654.

Voisey, Paul. *Vulcan: The Making of a Prairie Community.* Toronto: University of Toronto Press, 1988.

White, Richard. "Poor Men on Poor Lands: The Back-to-the-Land Movement of the Early Twentieth Century—A Case Study." *Pacific Historical Review* 66 (February 1980): 105–131.

Widstoe, John A. *Dry-Farming: A System of Agriculture for Countries Under a Low Rainfall.* New York: The Macmillan Co. 1919.

Woelz, William D. "Metropolis: Death of a Dream." *Northeastern Nevada Historical Society Quarterly* 3:4 (Spring 1973): 3–17.

Woodfield, Floyd J., ed. *A History of North Ogden: Beginnings to 1985.* Ogden: Empire Printing Co., 1986.

Index

.